Real-Life
CRIMES
...and how they were solved

Shreds of Evidence

CHANCELLOR
PRESS

First published in Great Britain in 1994 by Chancellor Press
an imprint of Reed Consumer Books Limited
Michelin House
81 Fulham Road
London SW3 6RB
and Auckland, Melbourne, Singapore and Toronto

by arrangement with Eaglemoss Publications Ltd

The material in this book first appeared in partwork form

ISBN 1 85152 594 7

A CIP catalogue record for this book is available at the British Library

Printed and bound in Hong Kong
Produced by Mandarin Offset

Picture Acknowledgements
Thanks to the following individuals, libraries and picture agencies for supplying pictures: **Front cover:** *(main)* Rex Features; *(left)* West Mercia Police; *(right)* Midsummer Books. **Inside pages:** Aerospace Publishing Ltd; AP WideWorld; Associated Press; Avon & Somerset Constabulary; Bruce Coleman Ltd; Continental Airlines; Ernest Dudley; Richard Whittington Egan; Evening Standard; Guy's Hospital; HM Customs & Excise; Hulton Deutsch Collection; Derek Ive; John Frost Newspapers; Kentish Times; Metro Dade Medical Examiner's Office, Miami; Midsummer Books Ltd; NHPA; Paul Popper; Photo News Ltd; Press Association; Solo Syndication; Syndication International; Dr Richard Souviron/Tampa Bay Police Department; The Tampa Tribune; Topham Picture Source; UPI Bettmann; West Mercia Police; Zefa.

CONTENTS

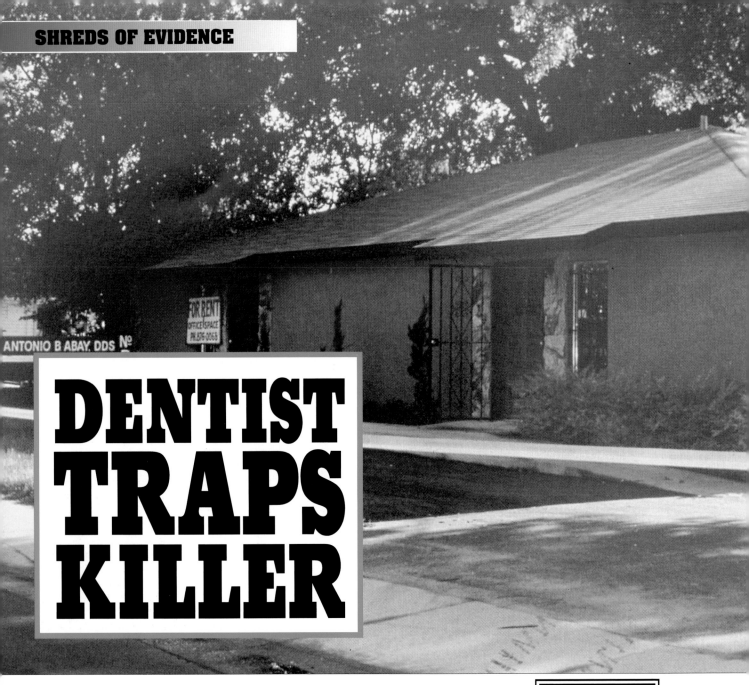

ANTONIO B ABAY. DDS Nº

DENTIST TRAPS KILLER

It started as the kind of mugging so common on the streets of Florida. But the attack on Barbara Grams ended tragically. It took a combination of pure chance and good forensic work to eventually catch her murderer.

Young Barbara Grams was assistant manager at The Hot Potato, a fast-food restaurant in downtown Tampa, south-west Florida. Work finished late as usual on Wednesday 17 August 1983. It was a hot and humid Florida night, and Barbara decided to walk from the restaurant in the Tampa Bay Centre to her home at 2911 North Boulevard.

Exactly 10 blocks from her home the 19-year-old was accosted by three men who tried to snatch her bag. But it seems Barbara recognised one of her assailants, because the criminals panicked. They dragged the struggling girl into a parking lot, and the mugging turned to rape and murder.

Her body was found the next morning behind 3911 North Boulevard. She was

Above: The body of Barbara Grams was found in the back yard of this dental surgery at 3911 North Boulevard, Tampa. The 19-year-old had been on her way home from the fast food restaurant where she worked when she was assaulted and killed by muggers.

lying on her back, her clothing pulled up, and her face battered and bloody with gruesome wounds to the chin and eye area. On her left cheek was the clear imprint of a savage human bite. It is ironic that 3911 North Boulevard was a dental surgery, because it would be forensic dentistry that would lead police to one of Barbara Grams' attackers.

The Medical Examiner said death had been caused by two blows to the head,

Not tourist Florida

Set on Tampa Bay on the Gulf of Mexico coast in Florida, Tampa is a major industrial centre and the seventh largest port in the US. Busch and Schlitz both have breweries there, and it is the centre of the cigar-rolling industry originally started by Cubans in the Ybor City section of East Tampa.

Despite its proximity to the beach resorts of the Gulf coast, Tampa is not a holiday resort: Tampa Bay itself is too polluted to permit swimming.

Right: Tampa has boomed over the last 20 years. The downtown area, where Barbara Grams worked, has plenty of office plazas and shopping malls. But like all industrial cities in the United States, Tampa has a high crime rate – in which Barbara sadly became just another statistic.

probably from a piece of timber, and that the bite mark on her cheek had been made around the time of death. The police brought in a local dentist to look at the bite mark, and he told them he thought it had been made by someone missing quite a few front teeth.

Suspect in custody

It was not long before the police had a suspect. Not only was he missing several front teeth, but he had bite marks on his body which he claimed his girlfriend had made. The police decided to call in an expert. They contacted Richard Souviron, the 48-year-old Coral Gables dentist, who had become well-known in Florida as a bite-mark expert. But Souviron did not come up with the answer the Tampa detectives wanted.

After examining casts of the suspect's teeth, Souviron was able to say that he could not possibly have made the mark on Barbara Grams' cheek. From comparisons with a cast of the man's girlfriend's teeth, he was also able to confirm the suspect's story about how he had got the marks on his own body. The man was released, and the investigation was back to square one.

The police, however, were not short of new suspects. Barbara's live-in boyfriend was high on a list that at one time numbered 18. So they decided to send wax

Barbara Grams, seen here at the age of 15 in a ninth-grade school photo, lived about 10 blocks from where she died. After leaving high school, Barbara began working at The Hot Potato fast food restaurant in downtown Tampa. Within two years the 19-year-old had worked her way up to become assistant manager at the busy establishment.

impressions of her boyfriend's teeth, together with those of two other prime suspects, to Souviron for analysis. The way the detectives told the story later, when they had finished packing these three sets of dental impressions, "there was extra room in the box". So they picked on a "dirtbag", a known purse-snatcher who operated in the area, and included a beeswax impression of his teeth in the

box. His name was Robert Earl DuBoise.

Souviron started work on the new batch of samples. He was soon able to exclude the three prime suspects. Then he took a look at the fourth set of tooth impressions marked simply 'RDB'. On 21 October Souviron called the Tampa detectives to tell them that RDB was their man. By pure chance, the police had stumbled upon the killer.

Arrested for murder

Souviron also said he needed a proper stone cast of DuBoise's teeth before he could be certain. The police picked up DuBoise at 2 a.m. on 22 October and brought him in for questioning. At 5 a.m. he was officially arrested for the murder of Barbara Grams.

DuBoise began screaming and kicking, and had to be restrained with handcuffs and ropes. At 6.20 a.m. he was given 10 milligrams of the tranquilliser Haldol.

Later that day Tampa dentist Richard R. Powell took further wax moulds of

◆ DuBoise's teeth. DuBoise had volunteered to have the impressions made: indeed, he seemed positively eager. "Fine, go ahead and do it," he told police. "I'll prove to you that I didn't bite the girl. I didn't have anything to do with it." But a stone cast of DuBoise's upper and lower teeth would later prove quite the reverse.

Held in jail

After his visit to the dentist Robert DuBoise was transferred to a 16-man holding cell at Hillsborough County Jail, and it was there that he first came into contact with another arrested felon, Claude Wesley Butler.

A few days later Tampa detectives were in the jail questioning Butler on another matter. With that business out of the way, they went on to ask him what he knew about his new cell-mate, Robert DuBoise. Butler said he knew nothing about the man, except that he had mentioned a girl.

"If you hear anything," the detectives told Butler, "hear a conversation, call us."

It was standard police practice. Sometimes a criminal will unburden himself to another inmate, providing vital information. For two months there was no word from Butler, then in December the police got the call. According to Claude Butler, DuBoise had told him he "only raped the girl", but then "things got out of hand".

This was the version of the events of 17 August that Butler said Robert DuBoise had given him. DuBoise and his brother and a friend had accosted the girl on North Boulevard that night, planning to steal her

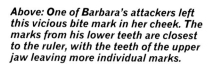

bag. She had recognised the friend, so they decided to abduct her. In the parking lot behind number 3911 DuBoise had raped her. While he was in the act, the other two had struck her with boards, and killed her.

Trial begins

The trial of 20-year-old Robert Earl DuBoise for the attempted assault and murder of Barbara Grams finally opened

Above: One of Barbara's attackers left this vicious bite mark in her cheek. The marks from his lower teeth are closest to the ruler, with the teeth of the upper jaw leaving more individual marks.

on 26 February 1985. Fingerprints found at the scene of the crime did not match those of DuBoise, and evidence from hair, blood and semen samples was inconclusive. So the prosecution case relied almost

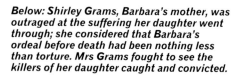

Below: Shirley Grams, Barbara's mother, was outraged at the suffering her daughter went through; she considered that Barbara's ordeal before death had been nothing less than torture. Mrs Grams fought to see the killers of her daughter caught and convicted.

Right: The police's number one suspect had only two teeth in his upper jaw. But the victim's cheek showed bruises and lacerations from at least three upper teeth.

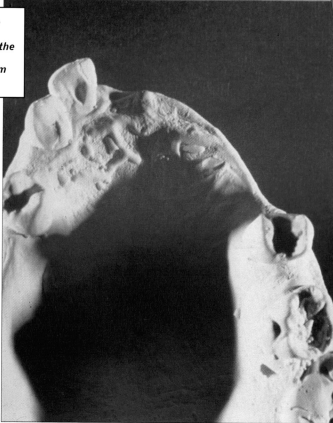

Working blind

Forensic odontologists prefer to work blind, not knowing who the suspects are, but evaluating the teeth of several possibles before picking out a match. It is then up to the police to decide if the forensic evidence can be supported by other corroborating evidence.

Beeswax impressions

From an examination of beeswax impressions of DuBoise's teeth, Richard Souviron found probable cause for a search warrant to be requested so that stone dental casts could be made. These show the biting edge of the teeth. Wax impressions cannot, and so are not regarded as scientifically sound enough to stand up in court.

The appeal court found that the original arrest of Robert DuBoise had been illegal because it was based solely on evidence from a wax impression. The defence argued that this should render the dental evidence inadmissible. But the court rejected this argument because DuBoise had agreed voluntarily to the impressions of his teeth being made.

The defence further suggested that DuBoise had been under the influence of a sedative when he agreed. But the court rejected this also. The dentist had observed no sign of DuBoise being drugged, and the 10 milligrams of Haldol administered by the police had had plenty of time to wear off.

entirely on the word of a felon, Claude Butler, and the expert testimony of Richard Souviron.

As for DuBoise's accomplices, the police had tentatively identified the friend, but there was no evidence against him or DuBoise's brother, so neither could be charged.

Juror disqualified

One juror, Robert Goodyer, had to be taken off the case, after he heard someone telling DuBoise's father in the corridor outside the court that someone else had told him: "I don't believe they have Robert in jail because I killed the girl." The third party mentioned turned out to be DuBoise's friend, but Judge Coe ruled that Goodyer could not testify in court to ▶

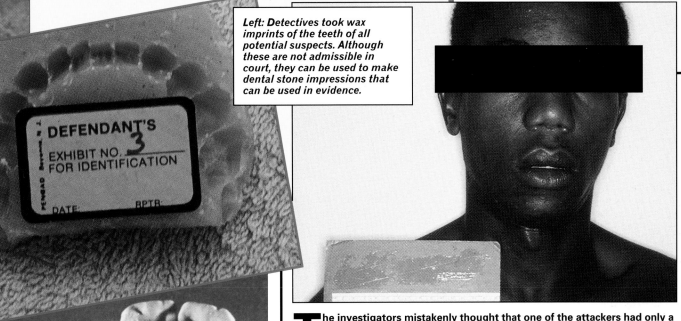

Left: Detectives took wax imprints of the teeth of all potential suspects. Although these are not admissible in court, they can be used to make dental stone impressions that can be used in evidence.

DEFENDANT'S
EXHIBIT NO. 3
FOR IDENTIFICATION

DATE: ____ RPTR: ____

The investigators mistakenly thought that one of the attackers had only a few teeth. They had been pointed in that direction by a local dentist, who was competent in his normal work but had little experience of forensic dentistry. As a result, they arrested a man (above) who had been in the area at the time and who had a previous criminal record. On examination, he was found to have bite marks on his own body. Could they have been caused by the victim? Or were they, as he claimed, from his girlfriend?

A forensic odontologist examined casts both of the suspect's teeth (white casts shown below) and his girlfriend's teeth (yellow casts). He said that the accused had not made the bite marks on the victim, and also confirmed that he and his girlfriend were telling the truth.

Identified by accident

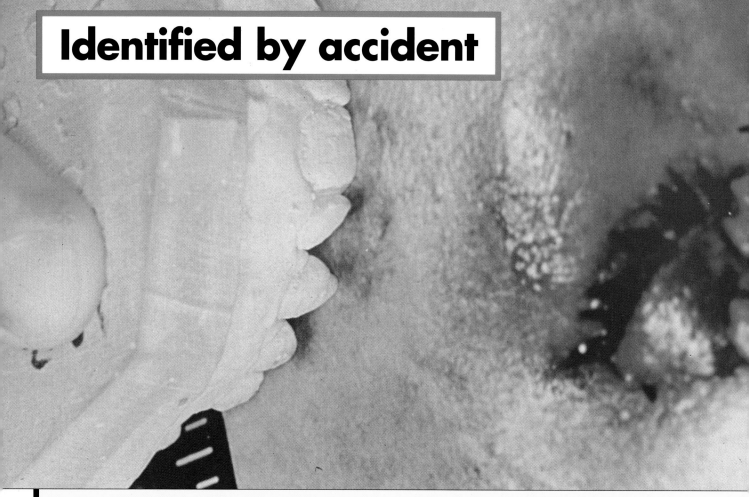

Dr Richard Souviron, a noted forensic odontologist, had been called in to examine sample tooth casts sent to him by the Tampa police.

"What was not reported in the newspapers," he recalls, "and what interested me, are some significant facts.

"Three of the four samples forwarded to me were high on the police list of potential killers of Barbara Grams. The detectives were fairly certain that their man was in amongst them.

"Extra room in the box"

"But Robert DuBoise was not amongst the suspects. His models and wax records were placed in the box of evidence because, according to one of the homicide detectives, 'There was extra room in the box'. They had discussed amongst themselves if they knew of any 'dirtbags' frequenting the area, and DuBoise's name came up. They asked him to bite into the wax, and he agreed.

"Had there not been room in the box of samples, had the detectives not selected a 'dirtbag' to fill the space, I would have positively eliminated their top three suspects, leaving them with nowhere to turn.

"But the incisal edge comparisons of Robert DuBoise's teeth with the bite mark on the victim fit the pattern."

"As was reported in the press at the time in their recording of the trial, I stated with reasonable certainty that Robert DuBoise did indeed leave the bite mark on the cheek of the homicide victim.

"Clearly he was one of the perpetrators of the crime, but there was no proof that he swung the 2x4 post which clubbed Barbara Grams to death."

Left and below: Robert DuBoise was quite willing to have a wax impression of his teeth made. It is possible that he did not understand just what a risk he was taking, not knowing what a forensic dentist could do with the material.

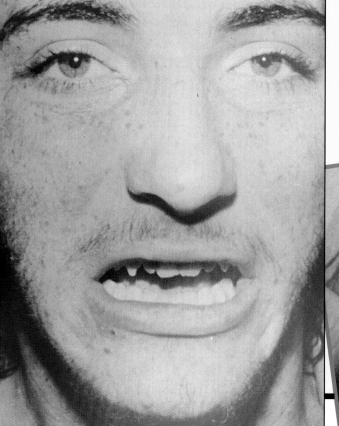

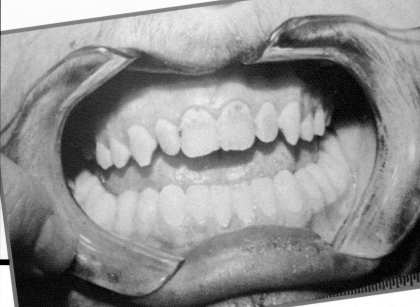

Left: Stone casts of DuBoise's teeth were presented during his trial. They were superimposed directly onto a photograph of the wound on the victim's face. This was to illustrate to the judge and jury the match found between the teeth and the wound.

the conversation he had overheard, because it was "double hearsay".

Myra DuBoise, the accused's mother, came into the witness box to testify for her son. In a confused and rambling testimony she declared: "Robert is innocent in the name of the Father, the Son and the Holy Ghost." She claimed that Robert had been home by 11 p.m. on the night in question.

Evidence is questioned

The defence then brought out that Claude Butler had been using psychoactive drugs in the cell at the time when he said DuBoise had told him his story. Butler had also complained in the past of hearing voices and of "seeing the walls melt". So with Claude Butler an apparently

Above: These are the four samples that were forwarded to Dr Richard Souviron to compare with the bite mark on Barbara Grams. He eliminated three of the four suspects beyond reasonable doubt of being responsible for the bite. However, two of the samples, marked 'RDB' at the bottom right of the group, did match. Souviron informed the police that he would need a stone cast to be sure. Further wax impressions were taken, and the stone casts made from these confirmed that Robert DuBoise was the culprit.

The Trial

Juror hears admission of guilt

Selecting a jury for any sort of American trial can be a fraught business. Both defence and prosecuting counsels can challenge the jury selection if they think it is unfair.

But the jury trying Robert DuBoise had another problem. One of the jurors overheard a conversation in the corridor of the court house. In it he thought he heard someone admit to the killing for which DuBoise was being tried.

In fact, the conversation had been between DuBoise's relations, who were relating what *they* had heard.

But by overhearing remarks deemed prejudicial to the trial, the juror was disqualified as an impartial observer.

Robert Goodyer was removed from the jury after overhearing the father and a friend of the accused talking outside the court.

Left: Judge Harry Lee Coe III, a former State Attorney for Hillsborough County, presided over the trial of Robert DuBoise for the murder of Barbara Grams. In spite of dental experts for each side presenting conflicting evidence, the state's version of events won the day.

untrustworthy witness, much of the responsibility for obtaining a conviction rested with the dentist from Coral Gables. But Souviron was not to have it all his own way, because the defence had found an expert of their own. Dr Norman D. Sperber, from San Diego, testified that, in his opinion, Robert DuBoise's teeth could not have caused the bite mark.

Souviron was in the witness box for four hours. His testimony was often complex and hard to follow, and he was interrupted constantly as the lawyers argued over which photographs he should be allowed to show the jury. But ultimately his evidence came down to the simple statement that: "The teeth of Robert DuBoise, upper

and lower, left the bite marks on the left cheek of Barbara Grams – to a reasonable degree of dental certainty."

Defence attorney Angelo Ferlita attempted to undermine the entire forensic case by telling the jury: "Bite-mark evidence is not a science as such. It is simply the opinion of the expert looking at the photograph of the bite, and comparing it to an impression of DuBoise's teeth."

Mercy recommendation

But the jury believed Souviron. After 14½ hours of deliberation they found Robert Earl DuBoise guilty of murder, although they recommended mercy.

► Barbara Grams' parents, Adam and Shirley, who had followed the trial from the front row of the public gallery, stood and hugged each other.

Angry at his conviction

As DuBoise was led out of court he kicked his chair, swore and slammed against a door with his arm. When he was brought back for sentencing Judge Coe tried to calm him, saying: "I know you're in a tough situation."

"You don't know how tough it is," DuBoise snapped back.

It turned out that DuBoise himself did not know how tough a situation he was in either, because Judge Coe then overrode the jury's recommendation, and sentenced him to die in the electric chair.

However, the sentence was later changed to life imprisonment by the appeal court. They recommended that DuBoise serve at least 25 years before being considered for parole. □

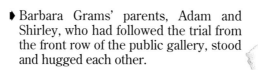

Dentist tes
he made i
of defenda

Whether the teeth o
the bite mark found
asked of a dental e

By BENTLEY ORRICK
Tribune Staff Writer

Robert Earl Duboise w
when mo

Above: Mark Ober of the Florida State Attorney's office was responsible for prosecuting DuBoise. Dr Richard Souviron was his star witness – the forensic odontologist's testimony was the plank upon which the state had built its case.

Robert DuBoise listens to the court proceedings. Even though he may not have wielded the bludgeon which smashed Barbara Grams' skull, he was sentenced to death for murder. This was commuted to life imprisonment when it became clear that the other people involved in the killing were unlikely to be caught.

Which dentist was right?

ies that pressions t's teeth

bert Duboise match a murder victim will be t in court next week.

your terminology, slightly crooked," he told Ober.

Duboise's court-appointed Angelo Ferlita, got at many per- bnormal-

In 1983 there were some 60 forensic odontologists, or 'bite-mark experts' as the lawyers call them, in the US. Some commentators believed that the two disagreeing dental experts cancelled each other out at the trial of Robert DuBoise, and that the jury must therefore have relied on the evidence of Claude Butler to convict.

Dr Richard L. Souviron, based at Coral Gables in Miami and expert adviser to the Dade County Medical Examiner, was the veteran of more than 200 appearances in court. Defence attorney Robert Nutter accused him of being "pro-prosecution", and of once having told a prosecuting

attorney: "You tell me that's the guy who did it, and I'll go into court and say that's the guy who did it."

Souviron complained that his remarks were being taken out of context, and pointed out that he had hardly toed the police line in the Barbara Grams case. He had actually obliged the police to let their first suspect go, and had then ruled out three more of their prime suspects.

"Too many inconsistencies"

For the defence, Dr Norman D. Sperber, ex-chairman of the American Board of Forensic Odontology, said there were "too many inconsistencies" between the bite mark and the cast of DuBoise's teeth, and so it could not have been DuBoise who bit the girl.

With the jury sent out of court the two experts clashed dramatically in front of Judge Coe. At one point Sperber rolled up his sleeve and 'bit' his own arm with models of DuBoise's teeth to try to prove a point.

In his final address to the jury Angelo Ferlita for the defence mocked Souviron, who had been instrumental in getting the conviction of serial killer Ted Bundy, as "the great Super-Tooth that the state brought in here". But ultimately the jury found Souviron more convincing than Sperber.

St. Petersburg Times

Judge condemns man convicted of clubbing teen-ager to death

KLEIN
rg Times Staff Writer

PA — Robert Earl Duboise emned to death Thursday urder of a 19-year-old Tam- n who was attacked, bitten bbed to death with a four as she walked home rk.

e Harry Lee Coe III sen- Duboise to death in the elec- air even though the jurors ously recommended life im- ent.

ley Grams, the victim's moth- ked Coe for his decision.

is could have been the only The jury could not have real- e horror that my daughter

went through," said Mrs. Grams, who along with her husband watched the entire trial from a front row seat. "Her body was torn apart. She was tortured. I'm glad Judge Coe realized what she went through."

The 20-year-old Duboise, who psychologists said has an IQ of about 80, kicked his arm again guilty ve

TH day afte eration later, L courtr of the t

Another bite-mark expert disputes earlier testimony

By HOWARD TROXLER
Tribune Staff Writer

A California bite-mark expert testified Tuesday that the teeth of Robert Earl Du- boise contain "too many inconsistencies" to have made the bite left on a 19-year-old murder victim's face.

Dr. Norman D. Sperber, a San Diego dentist hired by Duboise's lawyers, contra- dicted the state's expert witness, Dr. Rich- ard Souviron of Coral Gables. Souviron had testified Monday that Duboise's teeth ma the bite.

As the trial bogged down of incisors and bicuspid cuit Jud out

Dr. Norman Sperber outlined three reasons he believes the bite-mark pattern left on a murder victim's cheek was not made by Robert D. s teeth.

Sperber took off his jacket, rolle sleeve and "bit" his own ar of Duboise's teeth to p "You can't m Souvir

The Tampa Tribune

e death of Barbara Grams. The that Duboise raped Grams and companions, who were not ck of evidence, killed her as e from work on Aug. 18,

ying to prove that Du- degree "felony mur- e law is a killing another serious l battery. death pen- ant State

Attorney Mark A. Ober has said.
The trial pits the opinions of two leadi experts in the field of forensic odontol against each other.

Souviron, 48, of Coral Gables, has a dentist for 25 years, and has been ated with the Dade County medical ex- er's office since the early 1970s.

Souviron was the lead dentist in the 1979 case in which Ted Bundy was con- victed of murder on the strength of bite- mark evidence. He has testified in more than 200 bite-mark cases, he said.

Sperber, 58, has been a specialist in fo- rensic dentistry for more than 20 years, and has been associated with the San Diego po- lice and sheriff's departments and the dis- trict attorney's and coroner's offices.

a Tribune

Robert E. Duboise is charged with first-degree murder in the death of Barbara Grams, who was beaten to death in 1983.

Expert: Duboise's teeth left bite mark on victim

Dr. Richard Souviron spent more than four hours on the witness stand, but his message was brief: The teeth of Robert Duboise left the bite mark on Barbara Grams.

By HOWARD TROXLER
Tribune Staff Writer

Armed with models of teeth, graphic color photographs and snappy comebacks, bite-mark expert Dr. Richard Souviron tes- tified Monday that he believes Robert Earl Duboise was the man who bit Barbara Grams' face on the night of her 1983 mur- der in Tampa.

Though Souviron spent more than fou

hours on the witness stand in Hillsborough Circuit Court — much of that time waiting while the lawyers objected to each others' questions — his essential point was brief.

"The teeth of Robert Duboise," Souvi- ron testified, "upper and lower, left the bite mark on the left cheek of Barbara Grams — to a reasonable degree of dental certain- ty."

B

The clash of the experts provided plenty of fodder for Tampa's court reporters. The case drew wide media attention, partly because of the brutality of the original crime, but also because there was a genuine dispute about the suspect's guilt.

GRAHAM BACKHOUSE

MURDER

IN THE COTSWOLDS

It was an unlikely spot for a bomb blast, a frenzied knife attack and a shotgun killing. But the idyllic Cotswolds farmhouse was the scene of all three.

Above and left: Widden Hill Farm had been a noted centre for the breeding of prize Friesian cattle, until it was inherited by Graham Backhouse. A former hairdresser, Backhouse revelled in the life of a gentleman farmer, but a change to arable farming had brought financial problems.

Right: It was Backhouse's difficulties with money which led to an explosion of violence in this peaceful spot.

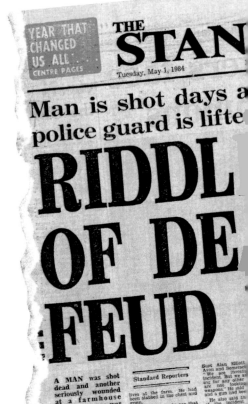

THE STAN

Tuesday, May 1, 1984

Man is shot days a police guard is lifte

RIDDL OF DE FEUD

A MAN was shot dead and another seriously wounded at a farmhouse which days ago was under police guard after a car-bomb incident.

The Cotswold countryside in the county of Avon is the epitome of rural England. But in 1984, these tranquil surroundings were the unlikely scene for murder threats, attempted murder by bombing, and finally a shotgun killing.

It all centred on Widden Hill Farm, Horton, near Chipping Sodbury, the home of Graham and Margaret Backhouse. A former ladies' hairdresser, Graham Backhouse had inherited the land and property from his father, a noted breeder of prize Friesian cattle. The Backhouses had been married for 10 years and had two children.

However, it was not all domestic bliss. Backhouse was a known womaniser, regarded with great disfavour by some sections of the local community. Others spoke up for him, saying he was devoted to his children, nine-year-old Harry and Sophie, aged seven, and also that he had provided a home for his widowed mother.

12

At the beginning of 1984 Backhouse contacted the police, saying he had received an anonymous letter threatening his life. He said he had destroyed the letter, which vowed that he (Backhouse) would pay for ruining the writer's sister. Soon afterwards, he told the police that he had received threatening telephone calls.

On 30 March he again called the police. His herdsman, John Russell, had found a severed sheep's head impaled on a fencepost with a note saying "YOU NEXT" pinned to the grisly display.

About a week later Backhouse handed the police an anonymous letter he had received in the post. It stated that the writer had been to the farm, but the 'pigs' (police) were about, and he would return. This letter was sent for forensic examination.

Car bomb

In spite of all this, life continued as normal at the farm. But it all changed on the morning of 9 April 1984. On that day Backhouse asked his wife if she would drive into town to collect some antibiotics he needed for the livestock. She agreed, and they left the house together. As she walked towards her car he reminded her that it was not roadworthy and suggested she should take their Volvo, telling her to drive carefully as it was a bigger car. Mrs Backhouse walked towards the Volvo, which was standing in the farmyard, and her husband turned into one of the sheds with John Russell to start work. Mrs Backhouse unlocked the car door, climbed in and switched on the ignition. The car exploded instantly, bursting into flames.

ARD CITY PRICES
Incorporating the Evening News

GRAHAM BACKHOUSE: knife wounds   MAGGIE BACKHOUSE: bomb in her car

TH ON ARM

A threat to kill

Left and above: When herdsman John Russell arrived for work he was shocked to find a sheep's head impaled on a fencepost. Attached to the head was a crudely scrawled note saying "YOU NEXT". Local gossip said that this was a warning to Backhouse to stop his womanising.

Below: The sheep's head was the latest threat in a 'hate campaign' against Backhouse. The police had to find out who hated the farmer enough to do such a thing.

Something strange was going on at Widden Hill Farm. A sheep's head had been stuck on a fencepost with a note, saying "YOU NEXT" pinned to it. According to farmer Graham Backhouse, this was simply the latest in a series of threatening letters and phone calls to him and his family. One letter had threatened the farmer for "ruining" the writer's sister. Since Backhouse had a reputation as a seducer, such motivation for a hate campaign was very likely.

A school bus was passing the farm gates at that moment. The bus driver stopped and, with the children, ran to the wreckage of the car. Mrs Backhouse had crawled out and was lying on the ground, bleeding from multiple wounds. One of the children, who knew the family, ran towards the buildings screaming for Graham Backhouse. In the shed John Russell had heard the noise, but Backhouse apparently took no notice.

When he heard the child shouting for him, he ran into the yard and tried to cover his wife with a blanket. She was hysterical and screaming with pain. An ambulance was called and she was promptly rushed to

Frenchay Hospital, near Bristol. Surgeons spent hours removing hundreds of lead pellets from her body.

Murder investigation

The police were called and began their investigation. The murder attempt appeared to be motiveless, but the previous pattern of threats, and the fact that Mrs Backhouse was using her husband's car, initially inclined them to the theory that Mrs Backhouse was an innocent victim – and that the real target was Graham Backhouse himself.

13

A car bomb explodes

Above and left: Just over a week after the sheep's head message, a bomb which had been wired to the ignition of the farmer's Volvo exploded when the car was started. Located beneath the driver's seat, the blast seriously injured Mrs Margaret Backhouse.

Margaret Backhouse was asked by her husband to collect some antibiotics. She took his Volvo estate – her car was not roadworthy. As she started the Volvo there was a terrific explosion. Miraculously Mrs Backhouse survived, although she was seriously injured.

The puzzle for the explosives experts called in to the investigation was to reconstruct the bomb. Made from shotgun shells and lead pipe, it was like a three-dimensional jigsaw. Many parts were missing, and those that could be found were twisted out of shape.

The powder from 12 shotgun shells had been packed around 4,000 pellets. The deadly explosive mixture was then put in to two sections of lead pipe, threaded together with a detonator and wired to the car's ignition.

Left: Although Mrs Backhouse's injuries were extensive and serious, they were not fatal, due mainly to the solidity of the vehicle in which the bomb was placed.

Forensic examination of the Volvo established that the bomb had been wired through the ignition. It consisted of two sections of metal pipe, threaded together with a detonator. The powder from 12 shotgun shells had been emptied to provide the explosive, and the device had been packed with around 4,000 lead pellets and was aimed upwards through the driving seat.

Plain-clothes police guards were now posted at the farm on a 24-hour basis.

Backhouse was questioned. Was there anyone who might have a grudge against him? He freely admitted to having affairs with many women, and said that any of the women's husbands could be suspect. He particularly mentioned a close friend who had been best man at his own wedding 10 years earlier. Backhouse said he had subsequently had an affair with his friend's wife, and the friend was an electrical engineer who could have the knowledge to make the bomb. The man was detained for questioning but was cleared of any involvement after several days in custody.

Another person put forward by Backhouse as harbouring a grudge against him was a neighbour who lived a few hundred yards from the farm. Colyn Bedale-Taylor, a 63-year-old retired personnel manager, had lived in the village for many years. In his retirement his hobby was repairing furniture.

Potential suspect

There had been a dispute between the two men over a right of way through the farmer's land. In addition, in September 1982 Mr Bedale-Taylor's youngest son had been killed in a road accident, following which the driver of the car had been acquitted of causing death by dangerous driving. Backhouse said he had befriended the driver and given him odd jobs, which had been resented by Mr Bedale-Taylor.

Nine days after the bombing, Backhouse appeared to fall out with the police and ordered them off his land. He said that if there was going to be another attack it would be better if it was before his wife left hospital, and he couldn't see it happening with police "crawling all over the place".

Backhouse told people that the police had advised him to be armed with a shotgun when he checked the farm, which he should do daily, to ensure that everything was locked up at night. The police later denied this, and in fact said they had warned Backhouse that he would be in serious trouble if he shot anyone, even in self-defence. Before leaving the farm, however, the police installed an alarm, which was linked directly to a police station on the fringes of Bristol.

Just before 8.30 p.m. on the evening of 30 April, the alarm sounded in the Bristol

police station. Minutes later, police cars arrived at Widden Hill Farm. On entering the house, officers found Graham Backhouse covered in blood and with deep gashes to his face and chest. Lying beside him was a shotgun, which had recently been fired. One slash on Backhouse's face ran from his left ear to his chin, and blood was dripping from the wound. Backhouse was taken to hospital and received 80 stitches in the main facial wound.

Neighbour's body

The body of Colyn Bedale-Taylor was found at the foot of a flight of stairs. He had been shot in the chest at point-blank range. In his hand was a Stanley knife which, it was assumed, had inflicted Backhouse's wounds.

Police questioned Backhouse in hospital. According to his story, Bedale-Taylor had arrived at the farm at around 7.30 p.m. Backhouse had invited him in for coffee and they had sat down and talked. Bedale-Taylor said he had called to repair a chest at the farm, and Backhouse said he replied by saying that the chest did not need repairing. Bedale-Taylor then said that God had

sent him, and why had Backhouse killed his son? Backhouse said that he was amazed by this, but suspicious at the same time, and asked Bedale-Taylor if he had planted the car bomb. Bedale-Taylor replied that he had, and would not fail again.

After seeming to pray for a moment, Bedale-Taylor pulled out a knife and slashed Backhouse across the face. Backhouse said he struggled free, and ran to get his shotgun, which was under the stairs. He then backed up the stairs, warning Bedale-Taylor to stay back. However, Bedale-Taylor kept coming forward up the stairs. "When the man came on, I became frightened. I lost control and fired the gun into his chest," Backhouse said.

This appeared to be quite conclusive. Backhouse had been pursued by a maniac with an insane grudge against him, who had

presumably been responsible for the whole campaign. Backhouse was released from hospital on 9 May and, with his wife beside him on crutches, gave press interviews, saying he was quite bewildered by the whole affair.

Meanwhile, the police investigation continued. The knife Bedale-Taylor had in his hand when his body was found had his initials B.T. scratched roughly on the handle. Police checked all the tools in his workshop, but none had been marked in the same way; special tools had been engraved with his full name.

The day after Bedale-Taylor's death, police found a length of metal pipe lying in his driveway. This appeared to be the same as the pipe used in the bomb, but it was not even rusty, so obviously had not been there long.

Below: According to Graham Backhouse, Colyn Bedale-Taylor had lunged at him with a Stanley knife. Scared for his life, Backhouse struggled violently, but could not avoid getting slashed. Running bleeding towards the hallway, he said he grabbed a shotgun and killed Bedale-Taylor in self-defence.

Story of a killing

When an alarm went off at the local police station, police rushed to Widden Hill Farm. Inside, they found 63-year-old Colyn Bedale-Taylor dead from shotgun wounds, and Graham Backhouse bleeding from several knife slashes.

Backhouse told police that Bedale-Taylor had attacked him with a knife. In the struggle, he had grabbed a shotgun, and shot the older man.

According to Backhouse, Bedale-Taylor admitted planting the car bomb and sending the threatening letters, claiming to have been instructed to do so by God.

Left: Police constable Richard Yeadon was the first policeman on the spot. As fellow officers sealed off the farmhouse, he saw Bedale-Taylor's body at the foot of the stairs, a Stanley knife in his hand. Nearby, Backhouse was found lying in the entrance to the lounge.

Below: Colyn Bedale-Taylor's body was removed from Widden Hill Farm the next morning for examination by pathologist Dr William Kennard.

Left: After the shooting at Widden Hill Farm, police searched Colyn Bedale-Taylor's house. They were looking for evidence that he was behind the attacks on the Backhouse family. The story seemed to be confirmed when a piece of the same pipe that had been used in the car bomb was found in his driveway.

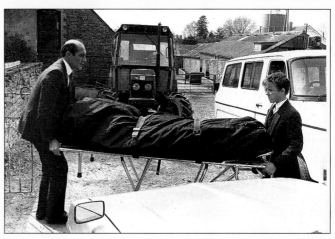

These small discrepancies were the first signs that all was not as it first seemed.

The next stage of the investigation was the recreation of the alleged events, using the evidence of the bloodstains found at the death scene. Geoffrey Robinson, a forensic scientist from the Home Office Forensic Laboratory at Chepstow, Gwent, was called in.

Shortage of blood

Most damaging to Backhouse's claim that there had been a struggle in the kitchen was the relative shortage of blood. Such a 'frenzied' attack would, according to Robinson, have left bloodstains of the 'splash' type on walls and furniture. In fact, quite contrary evidence presented itself in the number of *drops* of blood on the plastic floor-covering, indicating that Backhouse had been standing *dripping* blood.

It was true that chairs in the kitchen had been knocked over, but some had landed on top of blood drops, suggesting that the moving of the chairs was an afterthought.

One of the chairs had blood smears along the top (identified as Backhouse's, which differed in group from that of the victim), an effect that could have been created if Backhouse had grabbed hold of the chair with a bloody hand during the struggle and pushed it over. But if this were the case, how could a man who already had bloody hands have picked up and fired a shotgun *afterwards* without leaving a single trace of blood on the gun?

Furthermore, despite Backhouse's insistence that he had fled bleeding from the kitchen to the end of the hall, there was no trail of blood in the hallway itself – an impossibility given his injuries. All this led Geoffrey Robinson to believe that Graham Backhouse's wounds were self-inflicted, and that he had placed the knife in his victim's hand after death. Backhouse, he suggested, must have dripped blood around the kitchen after the shooting to simulate an attack on himself.

But when Backhouse had placed the knife in Bedale-Taylor's hand, he could not have noticed that the dead man's palms were completely covered with blood through clutching at his gunshot wounds. If Backhouse's story was true, and Bedale-Taylor had been holding the knife all the time, then at least part of the palm should have been clear of blood.

Self-inflicted wounds

These doubts were confirmed by examining pathologist Dr William Kennard, who expressed misgivings at finding the knife still held in the victim's hand: surely he would have let go when blasted by a shotgun. Also, Dr Kennard's view of Backhouse's wounds concurred with the self-infliction theory of the forensic experts. He confirmed that if the cut which was made diagonally downwards from Backhouse's left shoulder to the right side of his waist had been inflicted by another person, then Backhouse would have had to stand still and neither offer resistance nor try to protect himself.

On 13 May 1984, Backhouse was arrested at his farm and charged with the

---

Forensics

The wrong type of splash

The first hint that all was not what it seemed came during the forensic investigation by Geoffrey Robinson. Robinson, an expert at interpreting bloodstains and splashes at the scene of crime, had been called from the Home Office Forensic Laboratory in Chepstow. Straight away he saw that there was something wrong with Backhouse's version of events.

In a violent struggle, blood is flung about with great force. It makes a characteristic elongated splash. But the bloodstains in the kitchen at Widden Hill Farm were round – which would only have occurred if Backhouse had been standing still, allowing his blood to drip freely. Clearly, there had been no struggle.

Below: The bloody kitchen of the farmhouse was what might be expected from the scene of a killing, but there was something wrong. Most notably, the blood splashes on the floor were not the kind normally found after a violent struggle.

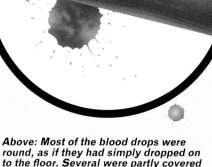

Above: Most of the blood drops were round, as if they had simply dropped on to the floor. Several were partly covered by furniture, but there was no blood on the furniture itself.

Below: If the blood had been flung around in a struggle, the splashes should have been a characteristic exclamation mark shape.

murder of Colyn Bedale-Taylor and the attempted murder of his wife. Following several magistrates' court appearances, he was committed for trial at Bristol Crown Court.

The trial opened on Monday 28 January 1985, before Mr Justice Stuart-Smith. Backhouse, who appeared in the dock with a ragged three-inch scar across his cheek, pleaded not guilty to both charges. Mr James Black QC appeared for the prosecution, and Mr Lionel Read QC for the defence.

The court learned that even after his arrest the prisoner continued in his efforts to incriminate Bedale-Taylor. From his cell at Horfield Prison, Bristol, Backhouse wrote to his wife, asking her to smuggle in

The medical evidence

Pathologist Dr William Kennard did not believe Backhouse's story. "The wounds *could* have been caused by someone else," he testified, "but Backhouse would have had to stand there doing nothing while his attacker slashed him from shoulder to hip. But with no self-defence wounds, I favour self-infliction. Also, the facial wound was of a self-inflicted type often seen in suicides, where tentative cuts are made before the major injury."

Threat to himself

Forensic examination of the letters and notes alleged to have been sent to Graham Backhouse showed that the farmer had written them himself.

Home Office document expert Mike Hall examined the "YOU NEXT" note. It had been torn from a spiral-bound notepad, and showed an impression of a doodle written on a previous page. When police searched Backhouse's office they found an identical pad, and on one of the sheets they found the same doodle. Backhouse had written the threatening letters to himself.

Above: The forensic reports on the wounds suffered by Graham Backhouse stated that they were consistent with being self-inflicted by a right-handed man.

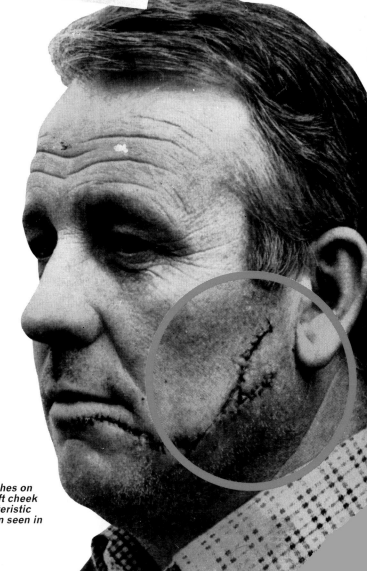

Right: The piratical slashes on Graham Backhouse's left cheek also showed the characteristic tentative 'trial' cuts often seen in self-inflicted wounds.

Forensics

A forensic conviction

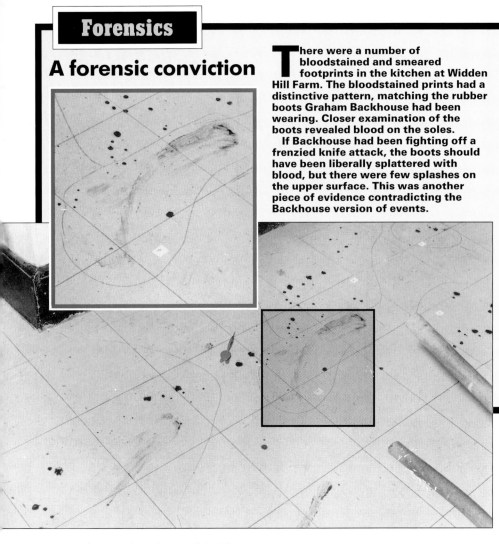

There were a number of bloodstained and smeared footprints in the kitchen at Widden Hill Farm. The bloodstained prints had a distinctive pattern, matching the rubber boots Graham Backhouse had been wearing. Closer examination of the boots revealed blood on the soles.

If Backhouse had been fighting off a frenzied knife attack, the boots should have been liberally splattered with blood, but there were few splashes on the upper surface. This was another piece of evidence contradicting the Backhouse version of events.

Above and above right: Some of the blood had been smeared by being walked on. The boot tracks in the kitchen had been made by Graham Backhouse, but not during a frantic struggle.

writing materials: "The police are fabricating evidence against me and my case is looking black. However, with your help I can improve the case considerably. I want to fabricate a letter to the press. So please help me. I must get out of this hell hole."

Letter to the press

The jury was told that Backhouse persuaded a fellow prisoner to smuggle out an unsigned letter, addressed to the editor of the Bristol *Evening Post*, which implicated Mr Bedale-Taylor in the bombing. Forensic examination proved that the handwriting matched the threatening letters that were supposed to have been received by Graham Backhouse, and that they both matched the handwriting of Backhouse himself.

Police had also discovered that the "YOU NEXT" note found with the sheep's head came from a notepad found in Backhouse's study; it matched an impression on the back of the note. The anonymous letter later handed to the police had also been examined by forensic experts, who had

identified fibres found stuck to the gum on the envelope with a cardigan found in Backhouse's bedroom.

As evidence of motive, Mr Black for the Crown questioned Richard Martin, manager of the Chipping Sodbury branch of the National Westminster Bank, who confirmed that Backhouse had accumulated debts of more than £70,000. The jury was also told that prior to 1984 Margaret Backhouse's life had been insured for £50,000. In March of that year, a further policy had been taken out for the same amount "in the event of her death or serious injury".

On Monday 19 February, the jury of eight men and five women retired to consider their verdict. After five-and-a-half hours, by a majority of 10 to two, they returned a verdict of guilty on both charges. Backhouse was sentenced to two terms of life imprisonment.

On his way from the dock, escorted by prison officers, Graham Backhouse passed within feet of his wife sitting in the public gallery; he did not even glance in her direction.

Below: Margaret Bedale-Taylor arrives at the trial of Graham Backhouse. She had suffered two grievous blows. First, there was the death of her son in a road accident – a death used by Backhouse in his attempt to shift the blame for his crimes onto Colyn Bedale-Taylor. Then Backhouse brutally murdered his neighbour and left Margaret a widow.

Graham Backhouse owed more than £70,000 to the banks, due to poor harvests on the farm, and the only handy source was his wife's insurance. The month before the car bomb explosion, Backhouse had increased the policy on her life from £50,000 to £100,000.

Graham Backhouse's elaborate programme of deception was designed to draw suspicion away from himself. When his wife survived the murder attempt, he felt he had to 'close the case' by carrying on with his plot to implicate Bedale-Taylor. Thanks to some superb forensic work, the plot led to his own conviction.

Left: Backhouse's farm had been known for its prizewinning herd of Friesian cattle.

Above: Although Backhouse still claimed to be a cattle breeder, his disastrous switch to arable farming was to lead to murder.

Below: Margaret Backhouse leaves court, where she learned the full details of her husband's plans to murder her and Bedale-Taylor.

Sharks are scavengers. They normally make short work of organic debris in the sea. But in 1935, one shark ate something that disagreed with him, and revealed a case of murder.

THE SHARK-ARM

A quarrel between Australian gangsters led to murder. But the crime was revealed in the unlikely surroundings of a Sydney aquarium.

The seaside suburb of Coogee in Sydney was packed with people on the afternoon of 25 April 1935. It was a public holiday, and the crowds were drawn to Coogee by the spectacle of a 14-foot-long, live tiger shark, caught recently by local fishermen. Until that afternoon, the shark had been something of a disappointment. Since its capture, the creature had refused to eat, bare its teeth, or even move about very much; in fact the spectators had viewed its sinister dimensions and moved on from boredom rather than horror.

Then, at precisely five o'clock, in front of the sleepy holiday crowd, the shark suddenly went berserk, thrashing wildly with its tail, snapping its huge jaws, torpedoing in circles around its tank. The audience gasped in horror as a dark mass spewed from the foaming jaws: surfacing from the slime was something so macabre as to suspend belief – a tattooed human arm, its fingers outstretched and a length of rope floating out from the wrist.

The vomiting shark presented an enigma to the authorities. It had been captured eight days earlier: could a human arm have remained undigested for so long?

Local shark expert Dr Coppleson believed that the shark had been in such a state of shock since its capture that it had eaten nothing; as a result the limb had not been broken down by the creature's gastric juices. He added that it should not be assumed that the creature had bitten off the man's arm. The wound was not consistent with the work of a shark's teeth – the limb had been severed with a sharp knife, and the creature had probably just taken advantage of it floating in the water.

Searching for the corpse

But what had happened to the rest of the body? In an attempt to locate the corpse, searches were made by beach patrols, div-

Above: Tiger sharks are dangerous and have a reputation as man-eaters. That reputation seemed justified when a sick shark in the Coogee Aquarium vomited up a human arm.

The question now was how had he died – and where, and in what circumstances?

Enquiries showed that Smith had been employed as the 'minder' of *The Pathfinder*, a fast little motor launch that had recently been scuppered by an underworld gang involved in the drugs trade. James Smith had escaped with his life, but was left without a job.

Suspected blackmail

The owner of *The Pathfinder*, a wealthy boat-builder named Reginald Holmes, was run to ground – and he seemed unexpectedly co-operative. Naturally he knew nothing about drug smuggling, but he did suspect that Smith was being blackmailed – by a man named Patrick Brady, owner of a seaside cottage to which he believed Smith had recently gone for a holiday.

However, when the police located the seaside cottage, at Cronulla, it was deserted. Their enquiries revealed that a mattress and a tin trunk were missing. If Smith had been killed at the cottage and dismembered on the mattress, a tin trunk might be a very useful receptacle. A boat belonging to the cottage had also been plundered of three mats and a coil of rope – a coil of rope matching the description of

Left: The Hobson brothers brought the Shark-Arm Case to public attention. Allen Hobson (with cigar) was fishing near Sydney when he caught a powerful tiger shark. He brought the fish in alive, and gave it to his brother Charles, who owned the Coogee Aquarium.

Below: The arm was so well preserved that a tattoo of boxers could be recognised. The question of identity was solved when police were able to record a faint set of fingerprints.

CASE

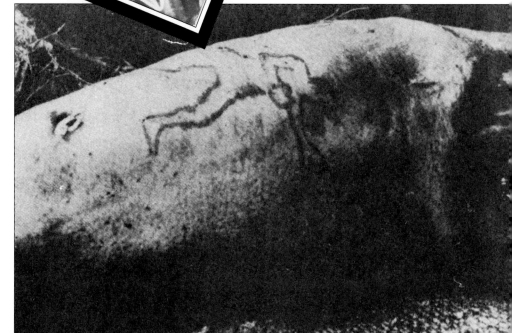

ers and the air force – all without success. Dissection of the shark's body also failed to reveal any more portions of the unfortunate victim.

In a delicate operation taking several weeks, the fragile flakes of skin from the tips of the fingers were removed and stabilised sufficiently to allow fingerprints to be taken from them. A search of criminal records revealed that the prints belonged to James Smith, described as "construction worker, billiard-marker, engineer, road labourer, and boxer; age 40." Smith was better known to the police as a forger and petty thief. His wife had reported him missing when he failed to return home from a fishing trip on 8 April. Mrs Smith later identified the tattoo depicting two sparring boxers on the severed arm.

The arm was identified as having belonged to James Smith. Smith was an ex-boxer, who worked on the fringes of the underworld as a marker in a Sydney billiard hall.

Arm Case would soon be laid to rest. But that optimism reckoned without interference from the twilight world of Australia's drug-runners.

A couple of days after the arrest of Patrick Brady a speedboat, wildly out of control, careered across Sydney Harbour. After a frantic chase by every available police launch, the boat was captured. Its driver, beneath a mask of blood, turned out to be none other than an hysterical Reginald Holmes. Holmes' story was that a stranger had shot at him near his home and wounded him in the forehead. Holmes had jumped aboard his boat and been chased by his unknown assailant in another craft, but he had finally managed to lose him.

Terrorised witness

No matter how crazy it sounded, it seemed that somebody was determined to put Holmes out of circulation by the time of the inquest on James Smith. Yet the police decided against placing Reg Holmes in protective custody, and after treatment for a superficial head-wound, Sydney's star witness was turned loose.

In the small hours of 13 June – the day set for the inquest on Smith's arm – Holmes' body was found collapsed over the steering wheel of his car; dead, with bullets in the chest and groin. The police had lost their witness, and with him, any chance of a case against Brady.

On its twelfth day, the inquest was halted by order of Mr Justice Hulse Rogers of the Australian Supreme Court who, drawing on an English statute enacted in 1276, ruled that: "A limb does not constitute a body," and a body had "always

that tied to the severed arm. Perhaps the killer had tried to cram the body into the tin trunk and, finding it an impossible fit, had lopped off one of the arms and lashed it to the outside of the trunk with rope from the boat; the trunk was then dumped offshore along with the bloodstained mattress, the severed arm eventually providing a shark's breakfast.

Pathologist's examination

Improbable as the hypothesis might sound, it certainly accorded with the known facts; it was also the theory favoured by the celebrated English forensic pathologist, Sir Sydney Smith, who, by lucky coincidence, was in Sydney at the time on his way to a meeting of the British Medical Association in Melbourne.

In his autobiography *Mostly Murder*, Sir

Smith had last been seen at this cottage on Cronulla Beach, north of Sydney. He had told his wife he was going on a fishing holiday.

Sydney described the results of his examination of James Smith's arm: "I found that the limb had been severed at the shoulder joint by a clean cut incision, and that after the head of the bone had been got out of its socket the rest of the tissues had been hacked away. In my opinion it was certain that it had been cut, and not bitten off by a shark. The condition of the blood and tissues further suggested that the amputation had taken place some hours after death."

In no time, Brady was in custody, held on a minor forgery charge; investigating officers at last began to feel that the Shark-

been essential for the holding of an inquest".

Three months later, Patrick Brady was brought to trial before Justice Sir Frederick R. Jordan. Hardly surprisingly, the case foundered without Holmes on the witness stand. Brady, in evidence on his own behalf, pointed a finger of suspicion at one Albert Stannard. Stannard, he claimed, had been at the cottage with Smith at the time of his disappearance. As for the attempts on Holmes' life, Brady had the perfect alibi – he had been in police custody at the time! Patrick Brady was acquitted.

Smith had gone fishing with 42-year-old Patrick Brady (above). Brady had a long criminal record for forgery, and was suspected of being involved in drug-running. When investigators learned that he was the last man Smith had been seen with, he was arrested on a fraud charge while they investigated further. Brady maintained his innocence of any charges, saying that if anybody was involved it was wealthy boat-builder and smuggler Reginald Holmes. Although police were certain Brady had committed the crime, he was acquitted due to lack of evidence. Even in his seventies (above right), Brady maintained that Holmes had been the guilty man.

Left: Reginald Holmes was Smith's employer. He told police that he thought Smith was being blackmailed by Patrick Brady. On the eve of the coroner's inquest into Smith's death, when he would have been a vital witness, Holmes was found murdered in his car, which was parked under the Sydney Harbour Bridge. Without his testimony, the case collapsed and Patrick Brady was set free. As a result, the puzzle of who killed James Smith remains a mystery.

In their desperation to salvage some dignity, the police authorised a £1,000 reward for information linking the murders of Holmes and Smith. But it was too late; a blanket of silence had fallen over the Sydney underworld.

Two further trials were brought at Sydney's Central Criminal Court, against Albert Stannard and his bodyguard John Patrick Strong; they also collapsed. At the first, the jury could not agree, and at the retrial Stannard and Strong were acquitted due to lack of evidence and their own unshakeable alibis.

Unsolved mystery

On 12 December 1935, just nine months after the file had been opened, the Shark-Arm Case was closed. But the rumours persisted. Perhaps Reginald Holmes had not been the innocent victim that he had played so convincingly; was it possible that he was, in fact, being blackmailed by James Smith? And why was he seen drinking in friendly – some said almost celebratory – fashion with Brady on the day after Smith's disappearance?

A question of identity

In most cases of suspicious death, fingerprinting will form a part of the post-mortem identification procedure.

With the corpse of someone recently dead, it is not necessary to observe any special procedures save to recognise that fingerprinting is more easily effected when *rigor mortis* has passed off, and if the body has been in cold storage, when it has thawed.

In the case of hands in an advanced state of decomposition or mummification, application should be made to the coroner to have the hands removed from the body for fingerprinting. In some extreme cases it may be necessary for the individual digits to be removed.

In instances where a body has become 'mummified', it is essential to soften the finger tissues before attempting to take prints. Soaking in a solution of glycol, lactic acid and distilled water is the usual procedure, although in some extreme case the process may take several weeks.

When the skin has become wrinkled by damp, one of three treatments may be used:

1 With a hypodermic syringe, injecting glycerine or liquefied paraffin wax into the bulb of the finger from below the joint.
2 Gently manipulating the tips of the fingers.
3 Removing the skin from the fingertip, scraping off the surplus flesh, and mounting on a card.

If the skin is peeling after long immersion in water, by cutting around the joint below the bulb the skin may be removed like the finger of a glove; slipped over the operator's own finger (over a thin surgical glove) it may be printed in the usual way.

Where the skin has peeled off flat, the underside of the skin should be carefully inked, since the reverse image of the ridges may still be intact here. The ink will enable the 'print' to be photographed.

A similar method is to take a cast in silicon rubber of the underside of the skin, which can be mounted and printed.

In some cases where the ridges seem to have disappeared with bloating, it is possible to suspend the dermis in hot Neatsfoot oil, which shrinks the skin to reveal the pattern.

Drugs are high-value, low-bulk products, ideal for smuggling by air. The cargo handling centre at London's Gatwick airport was one important link in the chain of an ingenious international drug-smuggling ring.

DRUGWATCH

'Mr X' was a suspected big-time criminal, who was thought to have been a mastermind behind the smuggling gang. It was his meetings with crooked Gatwick cargo handlers that tipped off investigators that a major 'scam' was happening.

Major successes against the drug barons are trumpeted on the news, but what is not told is that they are often the product of years of painstaking work.

It was early in 1987 when a special deep-cover Customs team first got wind that a huge drug-smuggling operation was in the offing. At their base in an anonymous office block in London, officers from the intelligence wing of the Customs anti-drug division studied the files and reports from their colleagues employed on the special surveillance teams. It was the beginning of an operation codenamed 'Revolution' that was to create new records in drug-smuggling history and end with some of the world's biggest racketeers behind bars for life.

There are only two ways that UK Customs investigators can crack the big criminal gangs. One is via information from the underworld. The other is by keeping certain criminal 'big fish' under routine surveillance in the hope that they will do something that reveals the nature of their criminal plans.

Operation Revolution started with a tip-off. The word was that a 'rip-off' team of crooked freight handlers was working behind the scenes at Gatwick. A 'rip-off' gang's technique is very simple. Smugglers make the arrangements for drugs to arrive by plane and ensure their allies on the ground are in position to allow the packages to bypass Customs.

A carefully planned undercover watch was kept on various groups of freight

Right: When 'Mr X' met Don Tredwen, investigators began surveillance on the new man. He was photographed meeting former gang boss Eddie Richardson.

handlers. For months no-one seemed to put a foot wrong. Then, out of the blue, two handlers were seen meeting a suspicious character who was already on Customs' target list of suspected drug smugglers.

The man seen meeting the freight loaders had all the qualifications of a major-league drug smuggler. Born in the south London docklands, a traditional breeding ground for many of London's toughest crooks, he had a long criminal record and had once served time for an armed robbery in the 1960s in which a wages clerk was killed.

'Mr X' now lived in a magnificent detached house on the south coast and drove a Rolls Royce. He was obviously wealthy yet had no job, preferring to describe himself as a 'general dealer'.

Now Customs had fresh reason to be suspicious. If 'Mr X' was meeting airport loaders it was a fair bet that he was one of a group putting up the cash to finance a big drug importation. And 'Mr X' knew lots of London's most successful villains.

24-hour surveillance

Customs began secretly to watch him 24 hours a day. He was followed to London, where he met another man in Blackheath. The second man was Don Tredwen, a 55-year-old car dealer from south London with a long criminal record and friends in the criminal underworld. He was suspected of being involved in a previous drug-smuggling operation.

Customs agent Hugh Donagher, the senior investigator in charge of the case, was now convinced a major job was being planned. He ordered his ghost squad of surveillance specialists to watch both men closely. But Donagher also warned his spy squad to be extra careful when tailing them. Villains of this calibre were certain to be highly 'surveillance conscious', and would expect to be followed by police or Customs from time to time.

They would take basic steps, like driving round roundabouts three of four times or making sudden U-turns, to try to ascertain whether or not they were being shadowed. They would probably also use radio scanners to eavesdrop on police or Customs radio broadcasts that might be describing their movements. If they became suspicious they might put the job on ice, or abandon the plan altogether.

Within a few days there was another interesting development. 'Mr X' and Tredwen were seen going to Gatwick airport together. There the 'Revolution' surveillance team, some disguised as maintenance fitters and drivers, saw their targets meeting two men, one of them named Bob Ritchie, in the cargo complex. Both were employed by a company contracted to unload baggage from dozens of international flights every day.

Ritchie and his friend were supervisors in charge of teams unloading aircraft luggage holds. They were in an ideal position to set up a 'rip-off' operation. They had a legitimate reason to be on the tarmac, and they could make sure they were the only ones present when any particular freight hold was unlocked.

All they had to do was know which bags from which flights to 'divert' away from the trailers feeding the baggage carousels. The bags, containing the drugs, could be hidden until the end of the shift, then casually placed in the boot of a car before being driven away from the airport as if nothing unusual had happened.

Waiting game

Surveillance is a waiting game. For 10 frustrating months nothing happened. The Customs officers were beginning to worry. Had their cover been blown? How long could they justify keeping this job running when new information about other operations was coming in all the time? If they stopped today, 'Murphy's Law' said the drugs would arrive tomorrow.

Then there was a breakthrough: the villains were going for a big one. Three hundred kilos of herbal cannabis, over a quarter of a tonne, had been purchased in Thailand on behalf of the syndicate.

It was packed and ready for shipment to the UK via a Dan Air flight to Gatwick. A

It was clear that the drugs were entering the country via a 'rip-off' at Gatwick's cargo-handling operation (left). Crooked baggage handlers would watch for a particular bag and take it off the baggage trolleys so that it would not pass through Customs.

The scope of the drugs operation widened dramatically when Tredwen and Richardson were seen meeting a white-haired South American. He was Antonio De Abreu Teixeira (above), a Colombian known to be a member of the Medellin drugs cartel.

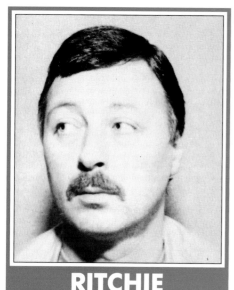

RITCHIE

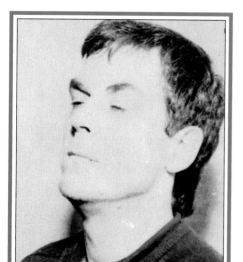

DEAN

Above: Baggage handlers Bob Ritchie and Tony Dean intercepted suitcases containing drugs as they were unloaded from aircraft.

check showed that Ritchie's colleague had booked himself on roster to be ready to receive the plane. A van had been obtained by Tredwen and parked in Surrey ready to go to Gatwick to pick up the load that should net the crooks more than £1.5 million.

Donagher's team were in a state of high excitement. When the dope arrived they would be watching. They would have the luxury of either making their arrest or covering the arrival with tight photo surveillance and waiting for the gang to make a second – probably much bigger – run.

Drugs seized in Bangkok

It was to be the climax of a year's hard graft. But then came the terrible letdown. Just hours before the anticipated sweep came stunning news. In Bangkok, Thai Customs agents had been running their own covert operation against the drug suppliers, unknown to their London counterparts. When the load arrived at the airport in Thailand to go on board the Dan Air flight to Gatwick, it was seized by local agents with pistols drawn.

But despite the huge disappointment of losing out on some good arrests, Customs intelligence agents were sure the syndicate involving Tredwen and 'Mr X' would try again. The conspirators had lost a substantial investment when the drugs were seized. Like gamblers betting on horse racing, drug smugglers who have lost their stake will often try to get it back by wagering twice as much the next time. Donagher ordered that surveillance of the prime targets should continue.

Two months later, a 'Revolution' crew were again tailing Tredwen when he had a meeting with another big-time villain.

The agent watched from a discreet distance as Tredwen drove to a scrap-metal yard, KWP Metals, in Deptford, south London. There he was seen meeting Eddie Richardson, long regarded as one of the true 'Godfathers' of British crime.

Richardson, then 52, had become notorious in the 1960s when, together with his brother Charlie, he had led an infamous 'torture' gang involved in extortion, robbery and every form of organised crime. The gang had used electric shocks to inflict punishment on people who crossed them.

Eddie had been sent down for 15 years at his Old Bailey trial in 1967. He was allowed out after only nine for good behaviour. Now he ran a thriving salvage business.

At first glance, he appeared to be a family man, married with two daughters and living in suburban Chislehurst. But Scotland Yard knew he hadn't deserted his old gangster ways. Most of his friends were professional villains, and the feeling within the police and Customs had been for some time that Eddie, like so many of his cohorts, was a heavy investor in the money-spinning drug-smuggling business. Now it seemed obvious that Richardson was also involved in the drugs plot.

Once again things seemed to go quiet until a chilly November day at the end of 1988, when the surveillance team struck lucky again. From a discreet distance they saw Richardson and Tredwen meet up again. They followed them using relays of unmarked cars and motorbikes as the two men drove to the Craven Gardens Hotel in Bayswater, west London.

Plans revealed

There more undercover Customs agents, posing as tourists, observed the two Londoners rendezvous with three South Americans. By using listening equipment the 'Revolution' team were able to hear details of the gang's plans.

Two of the strangers were believed to be Colombian, though research showed they also had Venezuelan travel documents. The third was Antonio De Abreu Teixeira, also a Colombian, who was known to use the alias Erik Schultz Ruyster. He was also known to the Drug Enforcement Agency in the USA and to British Customs and police as a 'sales rep' for the world's most notorious cocaine producers, Colombia's Medellin cartel.

If Teixeira was involved this was very big business indeed. It meant Tredwen's team had shifted their importation plans from cannabis to the addictive and much more lucrative cocaine trade.

The Customs men noted with interest that Teixeira had joined the south London underworld by buying a flat in Blackheath.

Richardson and Tredwen are seen outside the scrap-metal works which was the nerve centre of the UK end of the smuggling ring.

Making the deal

Right and inset: The British crooks and their South American suppliers met at the Craven Arms Hotel in Bayswater. They did not know that Customs officials were in the next room, using high-tech surveillance gear to eavesdrop on their illicit deals.

The Colombian drug cartel based at Medellin is a massive business, selling its drugs all over the world. It is run like a legitimate wholesale business, with 'sales representatives' travelling to make contact with various gangs and arranging bulk shipments.

Once Customs investigators saw Eddie Richardson make contact with three South Americans known to be members of the cartel, it was clear that something big was going down. By arrangement with the hotel management, a surveillance team was able to occupy the room next door to that in which the four men were meeting. By installing sophisticated listening equipment and wire taps, the investigators were able to eavesdrop on the conversation and establish that a major drugs importing syndicate was being set up.

RICHARDSON

Eddie Richardson and his brother Charlie had been gang bosses in south-east London in the 1960s. After a long prison sentence, Eddie had appeared to go straight but, in fact, he had simply moved into a much more profitable form of crime.

TREDWEN

Donald Tredwen was another long-time criminal. He was an associate of the Richardsons in their 1960s heyday. Although calling himself a car dealer, he was suspected by police of being involved in another drugs ring earlier in the 1980s.

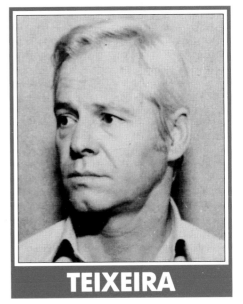

TEIXEIRA

Antonio Teixeira was well known to both the British police and the American Drug Enforcement Agency. He acted as a salesman for Colombia's Medellin cartel, making contact with and arranging drug shipments to criminals around the world.

His mere presence in the UK could only mean one thing: he had set up as a permanent agent or link man for the Colombian cocaine barons, with the brief to find customers in Europe and make all the necessary arrangements for shipment and payment.

Docklands meetings

The Customs undercover squad continued to watch as, over the next week or so, Richardson, Tredwen and the south Americans had a series of meetings at a flat in London's docklands.

The other two South Americans, Alejandro Alarcon and Edgar Garcia, then left London by plane for Venezuela.

While they were still on their way, Teixeira visited a print shop in Fleet Street and sent a fax message to Quito, the capital of Ecuador, apparently making travel arrangements for two people to fly to Gatwick via Frankfurt, Germany.

Teixeira was to make several more journeys to the same print business.

Customs later seized copies of faxes he sent to Ecuador showing cash received – $500,000 in all – from people referred to only as 'Ed' and 'Don'. This was clearly to confirm payment for cocaine received from Richardson and Tredwen.

On 30 November Teixeira went back to the Craven Gardens Hotel and met two South Americans, a man and a woman, who had arrived in London from Quito via Frankfurt.

Donagher's team had tracked their progress from half way across the world. They

Right: Customs played a waiting game, allowing the gang to bring in small quantities of drugs while waiting for the big one. Baggage handler Tony Dean was involved in another 'rip-off' from a Spanish flight at Gatwick. For some reason he took fright, and he dumped three cases in another cargo handling area. They were found to contain 50 kilos of cannabis.

Left and below: Cartel member Alejandro Alarcon met the drugs gang at London's Plaza Hotel. They arranged for a huge shipment of drugs to be sent from a warehouse in Ecuador (below), concealed in a consignment of balsa wood.

could be 'mules', couriers paid simply to transport the drugs. But they might be travelling light as a deliberate decoy.

Customs decided to play safe. If they moved to arrest them and they had no drugs, the gang would know they had been exposed and everything would collapse. They were later to learn that the Quito couple had been couriers escorting a 100-lb shipment of cocaine.

In December the Customs agents played another shrewd tactical move in their game of contraband chess. The Tredwen syndicate had ordered a tonne of cannabis to be imported from Morocco via Spain, hidden in a consignment of flowers.

Donagher decided to seize the drugs at Southampton. He knew he was in a strong position to arrest Tredwen and his co-conspirators at that point. But if he made no move, the gang might think it was just another piece of luck, and that no arrests meant the duty men did not know who was behind the importation.

Donagher rode his luck. He made no move to hit the conspirators and, confident as ever, they carried on with their outlaw operation.

Bags of money

Between 4 December 1988 and January 1989, Customs tailed Eddie Richardson while he made several trips to Teixeira's London hide-out.

On each journey he was seen to carry heavily loaded supermarket bags into the apartment in The Glebe. But Richardson was not delivering groceries. He was delivering a staggering £500,000 in readies, payment for the cocaine.

But without the cocaine, which was never traced after it left Gatwick, there was no point in Customs moving in to make arrests. Donagher and his team calculated that having waited this long, they might as well wait a bit longer. They knew that patience would prevail.

While all this was going on, other events were unfolding. In December 1988 an underworld friend of 'Mr X's' was scheduled to fly to Spain. The information said he was to return escorting a large haul of cannabis. Customs were sure the famous 'rip-off' routine was to be

employed once more. A tight watch was kept on the jet as it touched down on 15 December from Malaga.

Using some of the world's most high-powered binoculars, an undercover squad watched as two freight handlers, Tony Dean and another man, opened the hold of the Boeing.

Suitcases and other luggage went on to the trailers taking them to the terminal buildings and a Customs check. But the secret watchers saw the two men divert three cases and load them straight into a van.

For almost an hour the Customs team watched as the cases were driven around the airport. Eventually the crooked baggage men, nervous because they correctly believed that Customs were on to them, dumped the three cases in another cargo area and hurried away.

When the cases were not collected, investigators moved in. The bags were packed with over 100 lb of cannabis.

The investigators noted one other very interesting detail. The two baggage handlers who abandoned the attempt to whisk the cases away from the airport had both been on duty a few days before, when Richardon's friends from Quito arrived

with suitcases laden with cocaine. Another part of the jigsaw had just dropped into place.

It was time for Customs to take stock. They knew they had all the details of the main players in a major drug ring. So far the smugglers had successfully imported one load of cocaine and lost three loads of cannabis. Financially they were undoubtedly in the red, a great incentive to push their luck again.

Donagher firmly believed that by the very nature of the people involved they would go on with their enterprise until they succeeded in landing a truly enormous shipment – or until they got caught.

Police breakthrough

By the beginning of 1989 Operation Revolution was into its third year. But Donagher kept his team doggedly at it.

January was only a few days old when his faith was rewarded. There was an 'all ports' watch out for the two Colombians, Alarcon and Garcia, who had been seen meeting Richardson the previous November at the hotel in Bayswater. Now word had come from officers monitoring flights arriving in Britain that Alarcon had just re-

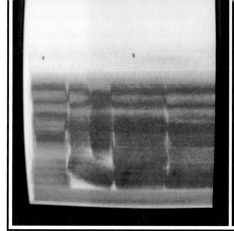

Above: *The container that was believed to be loaded with drugs was tracked from the South American coast to Le Havre in France and then on to Portsmouth. From there it was to be taken by road to a distribution depot in Southampton, where it would be collected by the gang. However, it was seized and taken to a secure area in Portsmouth to be X-rayed. The scan revealed something that was definitely not balsa wood.*

Above and below: *The centre of the load of balsa wood had been carefully hollowed out. When Customs men took the stack apart they immediately knew they had found what they were looking for. They discovered two tonnes of cannabis, worth nearly £6 million on the streets. Valuable though it was, the cannabis was merely packaging for 153 kilos of pure cocaine, worth £43 million at that time.*

freighter *Silver Happiness*. The searchers photographed the documents and then carefully replaced all the papers in exactly the same order they had been discovered.

Donagher's team traced *Silver Happiness* to a port in Ecuador. Among the containers it was taking on board was one loaded with balsa wood bound for Europe. The balsa had been ordered by a British-registered company called Globe Overseas Ltd. The managing director was listed as drug-smuggling suspect Antonio Teixeira.

Suspect container

By March *Silver Happiness* was bound for Le Havre in France, where containers due to be shipped on to Britain would be transferred to another vessel. Customs soon found out that the suspect container would be unloaded at Portsmouth, then moved by road to a distribution depot at neighbouring Southampton, where it would be collected.

Donagher needed to know for sure what was in the container and the check had to be done discreetly. If there were no drugs in this cargo it was imperative that the gang didn't discover that their goods had been tampered with.

On 8 March the container arrived at Portsmouth for routine Customs clearance. But this was to be more than a cursory check. The container was moved to a covered warehouse away from prying eyes.

A special X-ray machine was used and within minutes the duty men knew they had hit the jackpot. There was a large foreign object, something that showed up big and dark on the scan, at the centre of the timber – and it certainly wasn't more balsa wood.

With great care the investigators took the cargo apart. The timbers had been cleverly cut to leave a hollow in the centre of the stack. There the searches were met by a veritable wall of blocks of cannabis – two tonnes in all. And inside the cannabis 'box', a staggering 153 kilos – three hundredweight – of almost pure cocaine.

The estimated street value of the cocaine was about £43 million with the cannabis packaging valued at £6 million by the time it was distributed to small-time buyers. It was the biggest cocaine shipment ever to be intercepted in the UK.

The next morning at dawn, armed Customs raiding parties burst into the homes of Richardson, Tredwen, Teixeira and the other gang members as they were still sleeping. They were arrested. Operation Revolution was over.

Left: *In early morning raids the next day police and Customs arrested the whole gang. After a 13-week trial, Richardson, Teixeira and Tredwen were sentenced to 25, 20 and 15 years respectively, with minor gang members, like Dean, receiving sentences of 10 years.*

entered the country.

Undercover agents kept observation until he left his hotel, clearly intending to go out for several hours. With one surveillance squad tailing him in case he should suddenly head back to the Plaza, another squad obtained entry to his £150-per-night room.

There they found several interesting documents. They included shipping bills and import clearances for a cargo of balsa wood that had been sent to the UK aboard the Panamanian-registered container

THE ONE THAT GOT AWAY

'D. B. COOPER' AND THE HIJACK OF FLIGHT 305

Many aircraft have been hijacked for ransom, but only one man has ever got away with it. And the hunt for 'D. B. Cooper' continues.

The Boeing 727 sits on the runway after the passengers were allowed to leave. The car on the left is delivering the $200,000 ransom demanded by the hijacker.

Thanksgiving Eve, 24 November 1971, had been a busy day for domestic airlines throughout the United States. Most factories and businesses were closed, and in homes across the continent families were gathering for the celebrations the following day.

Gradually the rush of travellers going home for the holiday slowed. At Portland, Oregon, only 24 people bought tickets for North West Airlines Flight 305, an evening departure to Seattle-Tacoma. They would be joining the dozen passengers already on board. The plane had been on a long flight across the USA, picking up and setting down passengers at several different locations. Captain William Scott noted from the passenger list that his Boeing 727 would be less than a third full, with just 36 passengers for the final leg of less than an hour to Seattle.

Air hostesses Florence Shaffner and Tina Mucklow welcomed the small group of passengers aboard. They were the usual mixed bunch of business types in suits,

salesmen, accountants, one or two service personnel on leave.

The stewardesses paid no more than normal attention to the tall middle-aged man in a grey suit who walked the full length of the aisle and took one of the rear seats. Neat and respectable-looking with short hair and spectacles, he placed a large brown briefcase on the seat next to him.

Smooth take-off

Flight 305 lifted off smoothly, despite the wet and blustery weather. As soon as the 'No Smoking' lights went off the passenger at the back lit a cigarette. He pressed the buzzer for attention. When Tina Mucklow approached his seat he politely asked her for a bourbon and water. Ten minutes later he asked for another.

The stewardess noticed the passenger seemed a little on edge. He was chain-smoking, lighting a fresh cigarette as soon as he had stubbed out the previous one. Nervousness was not unusual. Even in the

age of mass air travel every flight contained people who hated flying. Many could cope only by taking a generous amount of alcohol and nicotine.

It was only when the passenger again pressed the buzzer for a flight attendant that the real reason for his nervousness became apparent. Tina Mucklow answered the call. As she walked from the galley to the rear of the jet she guessed passenger Dan Cooper was thirsty for another bourbon. She smiled down at him in his seat. He passed her a handwritten note. The smile faded from her face as she read: "I have a bomb in my briefcase. I will use it if necessary. I want you to sit beside me. You are being hijacked."

He then opened the briefcase an inch and invited the frightened stewardess to look inside. She could see what appeared to be red sticks of dynamite and wiring.

It was Tina's colleague Florence who was told to go forward and tell Captain Scott of the skyjacker's demand. Speaking calmly and precisely Cooper told her: "Tell ▶

The hijacker surprised police and airline officials by parachuting from the airliner as it passed over the wilds of south-west Washington State. None of the shadowing aircraft saw him jump.

Evidence

Parachute expert

Detectives believed Cooper had served with a US Army airborne unit. Only an experienced parachutist could have succeeded with such a daring scheme.

The Boeing 727 has a rear exit that can be opened in flight. Subsequent US Army tests showed that it was possible to parachute safely from these steps.

Police believe that Dan Cooper must have been an experienced parachutist to have attempted such a feat. Thinking that he might be a former US Army paratrooper, they studied records of the US airborne infantry in the hope of identifying a likely suspect. But this was wildly optimistic. Given his apparent age, Cooper could have served in an airborne unit during World War II, but then so did thousands of other men, all of whom would have to be checked. And given that it was extremely unlikely that the hijacker's real name was Cooper, this was an impossible line of investigation.

'Smoke jumper'

Another theory was that Cooper was an experienced 'smoke jumper' – a firefighter trained to parachute into the zone of forest fires. The states of Washington and Oregon had hundreds of such men registered with various fire departments. None of them produced an obvious suspect. Scores of parachuting schools and clubs across the

USA were also checked. Investigators drew yet another blank.

Cooper must have prepared himself well for the jump. Detectives think he wore a parachutist's protective jumpsuit under his business suit on the day of the crime. Although the temperature on the ground that day was a relatively mild 40°F, the temperature at 10,000 feet when Cooper jumped was 7° below freezing. He had to have been wearing protective clothing, or would have suffered severe frostbite and exposure on leaving the plane.

Cooper's 'bomb' was never found. Investigators doubt that he ever had a real device. They think it more likely that the case was stuffed with gloves, woollen hats and other clothing, as well as survival aids and a supply of food.

They believe that Cooper carried with him both an altimeter, so that he could verify when the plane was at the right height, and a compass.

They also believe that Cooper had taken

time to study airports and planes. In 1971 security was still lax at many US airports handling only domestic flights. He knew he could carry a bomb onto a plane without being searched.

After the Boeing left Seattle it was followed by three chase aircraft hoping to spot where Cooper bailed out and landed. But Cooper had chosen an almost moonless night for his hijack, and took the precaution of having all the cabin lights turned off before he made his plunge. None of the other pilots saw him leave the plane. And no-one saw a parachute. If Cooper was an experienced free-faller and had plunged the first 1,000 feet before pulling the rip cord, experts say his parachute would have been completely invisible to those following above.

Army parachute tests

Doubts that Cooper could have parachuted safely from the tail steps of an airborne 727 were dispelled a few weeks later when the FBI carried out their own experiments, using an identical aircraft and a military volunteer, over the Pacific Ocean. The volunteer found that although the aircraft's slipstream stopped the steps opening to their full extent, they dropped down inch by inch as he walked along them. He was below the scorching jet stream from the triple engines, and at the aircraft's minimum speed it was possible to jump without being 'slammed' by a wall of air or striking any other part of the plane.

Stewardess Tina Mucklow, aged 22, answers reporters' questions at a press conference two days after the hijack.

"He seemed rather nice"

The hijacker was perfectly calm, but his threat to detonate his briefcase bomb and destroy the aircraft had to be taken seriously. Police chiefs at Seattle contemplated storming the airliner on the runway after the hijacker allowed the passengers to leave. But they could not be sure if he was armed, or if his bomb was real. They agreed to his demands, sending US Air Force jets to follow the airliner on its planned flight to Mexico City.

the pilot that when we land at Seattle I want the following things: $200,000 in used $20 bills in a strong plastic container, and four parachutes. Tell him that I have a bomb and will use it to blow up the plane if there are any attempts to trick me."

On the flight deck Captain Scott, his co-pilot and fellow crew members were at first incredulous. Was this some kind of joke? But it was clear from the fear on the face of the young stewardess that the passenger was serious. He did appear to have a bomb in a bag.

Hijacker aboard

Scott tried to work out exactly what was going on. The man had asked for cash and parachutes, so he must be planning to jump out with the money. What were they dealing with here? Not a political terrorist, it seemed. But maybe it was worse. Perhaps he was some sort of psychopath. Captain Scott didn't have the means or the time to find out. For the moment he would have to obey the hijacker's demands and hope the situation would be resolved without a catastrophe.

He radioed the Seattle control tower to inform them of the problem. There was little time to make contingency plans. Flight 305 was only half an hour from its destination. Scott was told to circle over the airport while the authorities considered what to do. They decided to give the hijacker what he wanted. At this stage no harm could come from agreeing to his demands; they could buy time without put-

ting lives at risk.

In Seattle there was feverish activity as police fetched bank staff from home to gather the cash. At the same time more police were contacting members of para-chute clubs and local USAF bases to try to find the parachutes Cooper had demanded. The hijacker had asked for two different types.

Meanwhile Scott circled his Boeing over Seattle. On board the jet the other pas-sengers had no idea of the drama taking place around them. The last thing the pilot wanted was for anyone to panic. It was im-perative that the passengers didn't find out that they were sharing the plane with a maniac who might blow them to pieces at any moment. Scott announced that a tech-nical problem on the ground was prevent-ing them landing.

After two hours he was informed that the money and the parachutes were at the airport. Using hostesses Shaffner and Mucklow to convey messages to and from the cockpit, Scott told Cooper his demands were being met. He asked him to remain calm.

"No tricks" promise

Cooper replied that as long as there were no tricks he would harm no-one. He continued to sit smoking endless ciga-rettes, one hand never leaving the brief-case in his lap.

On the ground at Seattle every available member of the police and highway patrol had been moved to the airport, but law

FBI agents continue digging along the banks of the Columbia River after the discovery of bank notes from the ransom. Despite extensive searches no further trace of the money or the hijacker were found. FBI officials are convinced he drowned.

Did he survive?

Only two real clues have ever come to light about the fate of Dan Cooper. In January 1979 a man hunting in the woods near the hamlet of Kelso found a red plastic warning sign from an aircraft door on the forest floor. The FBI confirmed it had come from the rear door of Flight 305, dislodged during Cooper's escape.

But in February 1980, more than nine years after the hijack, there was an astonishing find in the same area. Eight-year-old Brian Ingram, on a fishing trip with his family on the Columbia River, made the discovery. While scrambling down a sandbank he saw something sticking out of the silt. It was 12 mouldering bundles of $20 bills, about $4,000 in all.

Serial numbers recorded

FBI agents had managed to record the serial numbers of hundreds of the bank notes taken onto the plane in Seattle. They confirmed that the notes were part of Cooper's ransom. The bank notes were some 20 miles downstream from where experts had predicted Cooper would have landed.

The money provided 'proof' to people on both sides of the Cooper dead/alive debate that their theory was true. For 'Cooper lives' believers, the money was evidence that the skyjacker survived and hid the cash, planning to collect it later. For the proponents of the 'Cooper died' school of thought the soggy bundles of dollars fuelled their theory that his plunge had ended in the icy depths of Lake Merwin, which feeds into the Columbia River.

FBI theory

FBI agent Ralph Himmelsbach, who led the search for Cooper, is convinced he drowned. He said: "I think he fell into the water and his body lies on the lakebed somewhere, together with the money. During the winter torrents, some of the cash may have worked loose and gone downstream, where it finally lodged on a sandbank and was covered in silt – until the boy stumbled on it."

That view is shared by Richard Tosaw, a former FBI agent who employed divers in a fruitless search of the river. He said: "I think he went into the river. His body is probably still out there somewhere, in an eddy tangled up among a sunken tree or some other obstruction."

Above: Having ordered cabin staff to turn off the internal lights, and for the plane to dive to 10,000 feet, the hijacker leapt from the rear exit.

Left: Colwitz County Sheriff's Detective Bob Nix displays an exit placard from a Boeing 727 found by a hunter near Toutle, Washington, in 1979. The FBI confirmed it came from Flight 305.

Eight-year-old Brian Ingram (right) found $4,000 of the ransom money near the Columbia River while on a family fishing trip in 1980.

Hijack man bales out with £83,000

The daring hijack of Flight 305 made headline news around the world. No-one had ever succeeded in holding an aircraft to ransom and successfully escaping with the money. Newspapers speculated that he was an ex-serviceman or possibly one of the 'smoke jumper' fire-fighters trained to parachute into forests to extinguish fires.

ARNOLD ANDVIK, a passenger in the hijacked Boeing, is reunited in Seattle with his wife and daughter after he had been allowed to leave the aircraft.
UPI by Wire

A HIJACKER armed with a bomb apparently parachuted from a Boeing 727 airliner last night after squeezing an £83,000 ransom out of the aeroplane's owners, Northwest Airlines.

The airliner touched down in Reno, after a flight from Seattle, Washington, during which the pilot reported he saw the man sitting in the open back entrance with a parachute strapped to his back.

Earlier, the 36 passengers and two stewardesses from the crew of six were allowed to leave the jet in Seattle where the man claiming to have a bomb in a suitcase, was given the ransom and four parachutes.

He said he wanted to fly to Mexico City but was told the airliner would have to make a refuelling stop en route.

When the jet landed in Reno, police and FBI agents immediately surrounded it on a remo' part of the runway.

But after a short tir 'med the man'

RENO, Nevada, Thursday

information on a man named Michael Cooper. Smoke-jumpers are forest fire fighters who parachute into inaccessible areas. (Reuter).

**Evening Standard
25 November 1971**

love both sides

Mystery

Who was

Dan Cooper is the only hijacker in history who has successfully taken over an aircraft for criminal gain and got away with it. But who was he, and what became of him?

Whoever he was, it seems certain that his name was not 'Cooper'. The skyjacker gave that name when he paid cash for his ticket at Portland. As FBI man Ralph Himmelsbach pointed out: "This man had done a lot of planning to ensure he got away. It would be hardly likely that he would do all that and then leave us his true identity."

Armed robber

Some investigators believe he was a man from Utah who was jailed after pulling off another hijack in 1975, but who died in a prison riot. Others think he was former armed robber Bryant 'Jack' Confelt, who died in 1975 after a lengthy illness. Knowing he was terminally ill Confelt decided to confess to the FBI. Details of his story were convincing, but Confelt claimed to have jumped from the plane near Mount Hood, 25 miles south of the Columbia River. If that was true say investigators, how did bundles of the stolen cash get to be 60 miles away in 1980?

Another more recent theory is that 'Cooper' was former Sunday School teacher John List, now serving time for murdering his family. List, a middle-aged accountant, vanished in November 1971 after his mother, his wife and their three children were found shot dead in their home in Newark, New Jersey. The law finally caught up with List in Richmond, Virginia, in 1989, where he was living under a new identity. The FBI said they had reason to believe he may be Cooper, the air pirate. But List has never confessed.

A new identity

A book published in the 1980s claimed that Cooper was a man called Paul Cotton, who left his family and job to try to start life again under a new identity. According to the book Cooper broke his ankle on landing. Seeking shelter, he was taken in by a woman living in a small mountain hamlet. They became lovers and lived together off the ransom money until 'Cotton' died of a heart attack in 1982.

enforcement chiefs decided it was too risky to try to storm the aircraft. They simply did not have enough information to guarantee success, and the price of failure was too appalling to contemplate. Flight 305 would be allowed to dock as normal.

When the plane touched down, 35 of the passengers disembarked, blissfully unaware of the tense situation they were leaving behind them. Just one man remained in his seat: Dan Cooper. He instructed Scott to allow all but one of the cabin staff to leave the plane. Tina Mucklow must stay on board.

This was the moment of greatest tension for everyone involved. Cooper knew that if an attempt were going to be made to seize him it could happen only now, with

the jet on the tarmac. He repeatedly told the frightened air hostess that nothing would happen – as long as the authorities outside the plane kept their part of the bargain.

Bundles of dollar bills

Just before midnight Tina Mucklow was sent down the aircraft steps to receive from police the parachutes and the money, bundles of $20 bills packed in a heavy duty plastic laundry bag.

Throughout the episode Cooper never left his seat. The parachutes and the money were carried to him and placed on the seats on the other side of the aisle. Then Cooper gave instructions for the jet

to take off again.

As the 727 taxied to the end of the runway Cooper sent word to Scott to set course for Mexico City. Scott sent an urgent message back. They would have to land at Reno, Nevada, to refuel if they were to reach Central America. Cooper indicated that that was all right by him, and the plane took off.

Less than five minutes into the journey, with the aircraft still climbing, Scott received another message from the hijacker. He was to descend to under 10,000 feet, lower his flaps, and let down the undercarriage. Cooper wanted the aircraft's speed reduced to the absolute minimum. The drag created by the flaps and the landing gear would slow the plane down to a speed

D. B. Cooper?

Right: The Boeing 727 was ideal for the skyjacker's purposes because it had a rear exit.

Above: Artist's impressions of 'Mr Cooper' failed to prompt anyone's memory. He paid for his airline ticket with cash, and was undoubtedly using a false name.

Right: John List was a former teacher who was on the run for nearly 20 years after massacring his family in 1971. After his arrest in 1989 the FBI announced it was reopening the D. B. Cooper case, and some authorities believe he was the hijacker.

Below right: Dr Larry Lewman holds a skull discovered in a remote Oregon forest in 1975. It was thought that the remains found in the Mount Hood National Forest might have been those of D. B. Cooper.

Right: One theory about the mystery man's fate is that he injured himself when landing, and was helped by a woman who lived locally in a small hamlet.

at which a man could jump – and survive. The 727 could safely fly at speeds as low as 120 knots. Cooper selected one of the parachutes with a 28-foot canopy and strapped it on.

'Air stairs' escape

The Boeing 727 had one feature that set it apart from other jets then in passenger service: an exit at the rear of the fuselage. Under the aircraft's tail and below the cluster of engines was a set of 'air stairs'. When the rear door was open the steps could be lowered hydraulically. It was a useful device that helped to speed the movement of passengers on and off the plane, especially at many smaller airports without

Criminal legend

Dan Cooper became known as 'D. B.' Cooper only after a series of letters claiming to be from the hijacker and signed 'D. B. Cooper' were sent to American newspapers shortly after the incident. The writer claimed that he had planned his crime meticulously and that the law had only a short time to find him because he was terminally ill, with only 14 months to live. The FBI believed the letters were hoaxes.

Cooper fan club

The case of D. B. Cooper has now passed into folkore. Every November hundreds of trippers, many of them members of his official fan club, descend on Ariel for a party and to search for any trace of him. Local shops do a roaring trade in T-shirts bearing the slogan 'D. B. Cooper where are you?'

His story has featured in country and western songs and has even been made into a Hollywood feature film, *The Pursuit of D. B. Cooper*, starring Robert Duvall and Treat Williams.

D. B. Cooper got away with a small fortune and never hurt anyone in the process. He became an instant folk hero, and people descend on Ariel, Washington, every November for an anniversary celebration.

states of Oregon and Washington were in pandemonium. Someone had just got away with the most audacious act of air piracy that anyone could remember. But had he got away? If he had survived, could he still be caught?

FBI agents hurriedly debriefed Scott and his crew. Based on the speed, height and direction of the aircraft, it was possible to calculate that Cooper had bailed out close to the state border. The area was covered with dense forest ranging over craggy peaks, their caps covered with snow at that time of year. The countryside was some of the wildest in the USA. Home to bears, wolves and mountain lions, the vast wooded wilderness was rarely visited by humans apart from a few hunters, trappers and loggers.

The settlement nearest to where Cooper was thought to have dropped was

Helicopters of the US Army's 3rd Armored Cavalry regiment take off to continue the search for D. B. Cooper. The FBI called in the Army, and the cavalrymen set up their camp on the shores of Lake Merwin.

they were now flying at under 10,000 feet with airspeed down to less than 150 knots. At that altitude, the air pressure outside the plane almost matched that inside. The door could be opened without disastrous results.

Cooper's last message

Cooper's last message to Scott was to close the flight-deck door and keep himself and his remaining crew inside. If Cooper saw the door open he would detonate the bomb. The last Scott saw of him was through the cockpit door as it closed. Cooper was at the rear of the plane, strapping on the parachute. Somewhere over the Cascade Mountains he lowered the rear steps – and vanished.

Captain Scott, following the skyjacker's instructions to the letter, flew on to Reno. Cooper and the cash had gone – but could a man survive such a daredevil escapade?

As dawn broke on 25 November the

mobile stair assemblies or sophisticated docking facilities.

The steps were raised and lowered by controls operated by the cabin crew. The locking mechanism was inside the cockpit, to ensure the steps could not be lowered accidentally in flight. Cooper now sent word to Scott to release the locks on the tail steps.

Scott could see from his altimeter that

the tiny logging town of Ariel. For the next few weeks it became the centre of an enormous manhunt. Hundreds of police, state troopers and FBI agents with dogs and trackers set off into the forests searching for clues. Troops from the Third Armoured Division plus jungle warfare specialists, some just back from Vietnam, were ferried into the area. They were joined by hundreds of civilian volunteers, hoping to find a fortune hanging from a bush, and professional bounty hunters hoping to claim a 10 per cent reward for bringing Cooper in – dead or alive.

Overhead an armada of helicopters from the National Guard, the Army and forest-fire fighters searched thousands of square miles of forest, looking for a parachute hooked up in the branches of a tree, a splash of colour out of place against the greenery. But they found nothing. □

Soldiers and National Guardsmen joined police and hundreds of civilian volunteers in the hunt for the parachutist.

Soldiers comb forest

Cooper had parachuted into some of the wildest country in America: a mountainous wilderness with snow-capped peaks and dense forest. The nearest settlement to his projected landing site was the little town of Ariel. Unless Cooper had help on the ground, or was extremely well-equipped, it would have been difficult for him to escape. Soldiers and police patrolled the area for weeks, but they found no sign of him. Some concluded the hijacker had got clean away; others believed he died in one of the icy lakes.

Another hijacker was not so successful: Air Force jets shadowed the airliner and the FBI planted a homing device in the bag containing the ransom.

Copycat crime

Two months after Cooper made his plunge over the Cascade Mountains, a copycat hijacker took over a jet at Las Vegas, Nevada. The man used an identical bomb plot to get $50,000 and two parachutes brought on board, in exchange for freeing 67 passengers and two hostesses. But when he lowered the rear stairs and jumped out with his loot near Denver, he plunged straight into the hands of waiting sheriffs.

Homing beacon

FBI agents, learning from the Cooper case, had slipped a small homing beacon into the bag containing the cash. And two F-111 fighter planes, scrambled to follow the hijacked DC-9, were able to circle the hijacker as he floated down into a field.

Bank Raid Murder

Above: Bank clerk Angela Wooliscroft lived with her parents in Chessington, Surrey. An athletic girl, aged 20, she was a very good hockey player and had been selected to represent Barclays Bank.

Above: At 12.30 p.m. on 10 November 1976 a man approached the till behind which Angela was working. Brandishing a sawn-off shotgun, he demanded money. Angela obeyed his instructions and placed the cash in the tray, but seconds later the shotgun went off, and Angela lay dying.

Angela had worked at Barclays Bank on Upper Ham Road (left) for four years. Ham is a prosperous suburb south west of London, between Richmond and Kingston.

It seemed like a typical armed raid on a suburban bank. But with one needless blast of a shotgun, the criminal turned a robbery into brutal murder.

The morning of 10 November 1976 was cold and overcast when 20-year-old bank clerk Angela Wooliscroft left her home in Chessington, Surrey, and headed for work. She was in high spirits. An outstanding hockey player, she was due to fly off to Jersey the next day to play for Barclays Bank in a tournament. But tragedy was about to strike.

As she parked her Ford Cortina near the branch where she worked in Upper Ham Road, Richmond, her eventual killer was also setting out for work. For 37-year-old villain Michael Hart, 'work' meant crime – in this case armed robbery.

Hart, who lived in Basingstoke, Hampshire, was a desperate man. With a long record of violent crime behind him, Hart was already on bail, despite strong police objections, for a jewel robbery.

He also knew detectives in Hampshire were looking into nearly 50 other robberies and burglaries they suspected him of doing. Worse, detectives in Paris were trying to get him extradited to France to face charges of the attempted murder of a policeman in an amazing shoot-out near the Charles de Gaulle airport two months earlier.

After a row over an unpaid fare, Hart had attacked a taxi driver with a knife, seriously wounding him. When five gendarmes had tried to arrest him, he had snatched a pistol from one and opened fire. All the shots missed.

Escaped arrest

Despite a huge search and all-ports watch, he had still managed to get away. But the French knew exactly who they wanted and had contacted Interpol to have their suspect tracked down in Britain.

Hart was expecting to go to jail for a long stretch. He wanted to ensure that if he did he had a large cash reserve stashed away for when he came out. He had 'cased' a number of banks in London and the Home Counties and had eventually settled on Barclays' Richmond branch as an ideal target.

Disguised with a dark wig and brown make-up in the hope of being mistaken for an Asian, Hart pulled up outside the bank in a stolen Austin just before 12.30 p.m.

Covering the barrels of a sawn-off shotgun with a raincoat, he walked straight into the bank and up to Angela's counter. He thrust the gun barrels against her protective screen and growled at the terrified ▶

clerk to hand over the cash.

Fighting her fear, and too far away to reach a hidden alarm button, Angela did what she was told. She took a bundle of notes and placed them in the tray in front of her. It was the last thing she ever did.

As Hart scooped up the money – about £2,000 – there was a deafening explosion as he let fly with the gun. At such close range even the toughened glass was no defence. It shattered, and Angela was hit in the face and throat.

As she slumped to the floor, fatally wounded, Hart ran from the bank. And, as colleagues and ambulance crews fought in vain to stop Angela from bleeding to death from a severed artery in her throat, Hart was calmly driving his stolen getaway car back to the multi-storey car park in Kingston-upon-Thames from where he had taken it.

The car the killer used was stolen from the Bentalls store car park in Kingston-upon-Thames. After the robbery Hart calmly returned it and swapped to his own car.

Transferring to his own car to drive home, he made a detour to the Thames near Hampton Court, where he threw the gun in the river.

A post-mortem performed by Keith Mant, Professor of Forensic Medicine at London's Guy's Hospital, told the horrific

Reconstruction

To catch a killer

1 SHOTGUN BLAST: Michael Hart shot Angela Wooliscroft with a sawn-off shotgun. He was later to claim that the gun had gone off accidentally.

The senseless murder of a young woman aroused great public anger. Extensive press coverage, together with a £50,000 reward offered by Barclays Bank, ensured that a police appeal for assistance generated a mass of leads.

YOUR ATTENTION IS DRAWN TO THE CARS BESIDE BARCLAYS BANK DID ANYONE on 10-11-76 SEE THE RED AUSTIN. UJD 362F, PARKED ANYWHERE IN THIS AREA.

METROPOLITAN POLICE
Appeal for Witnesses
MURDER

ANGELA WOOLISCROFT, aged 20
WED 10 NOVEMBER, 12.30 pm
Barclays Bank, Upper Ham Road, Ham, Richmond
She was shot during a robbery in which £2,500 was stolen.

DID YOU SEE ANYTHING?
Please contact the Murder Squad at
RICHMOND POLICE STATION
Tel: **01-940 9595**
All information treated as strictly confidential

story of what actually killed Angela. The gun blast had punched through the triple glass safety screen and, at such close range, the bulk of the shot had not even started to spread before tearing a wound an inch in diameter in her throat, rupturing the left carotid artery.

Hunt for the killer

Detectives assigned to the hunt for Angela's killer were sure the shooting was the work of a professional villain, not a one-off amateur, and started checking scores of robbery suspects in London and the Home Counties.

It was nearly two weeks before they started to scrutinise Hart. Thirteen days after the shooting, an alarm went off following a break-in at Jackson's Garage in Basingstoke at two in the morning.

When he was recognised after an attempted robbery at Jackson's Garage, Hart went on the run, after ditching his car and escaping across fields.

As two constables answering the 999 alert sped towards the garage in their Rover patrol car they saw a blue Ford Consul, with its lights off, roar away from the forecourt and flash past in the opposite direction.

Flinging their car into a 180-degree turn, constables Ian McIlwraith and Steven Mycock gave chase at speeds topping 100 mph. After several miles the Ford screeched out of control and crashed.

The driver ran off across the darkened fields. He escaped, but both pursuing policemen recognised Michael Hart, a well-known local criminal.

It was the contents of the car that made Hart a very wanted man indeed. A .22 French-made Hendaye automatic pistol with 72 rounds of ammunition topped the list, closely followed by stolen jewellery, several stolen driving licences and some disguises.

The pistol had been stolen in a burglary at a gun dealer's business in Reading. A Webley revolver, an 80-year-old Reilly shotgun and some boxes of number seven Eley trap-shooting cartridges had also been taken.

Important discovery

Within hours, detectives had a warrant to search Hart's house in St Peters Road, Basingstoke. Hart had already fled, but his wife Maureen was at home when the CID called. The detectives were quickly rewarded for their efforts. Hidden under the stairs, with a hoard of miscellaneous stolen goods, were 19 shotgun cartridges from the batch stolen in Reading.

Chief Superintendent Sewell already had a hunch that Hart was the wanted gunman. But there was one big problem. Forensic tests had proved that Angela had been killed with number seven game shot.

The shells at Hart's home were loaded with much harder, entirely different trap shot used by clay pigeon enthusiasts. At least, according to the label they were. Could there have been a mistake at the factory?

Sewell took out a penknife and opened one of the cartridges. As he removed the wadding, bird shot – identical to that used to kill Angela – pattered across his desk at Scotland Yard. The lab took only two hours to confirm Sewell's hunch.

How could it have happened? The detective went to the factory where the shotgun cartridges had been made. Yes, there had been a million-to-one mistake. A computer error meant that a batch of game cartridges had been wrongly labelled as trap shells.

Cartridge clue

The pellets were the clue that would be Hart's undoing. Sewell immediately issued a force-wide order: "Find Hart – bring him to me."

But where was he? The detectives knew he hadn't gone far. Hart, desperate for cash, had been trying to collect some 'straight' money he had actually earned honestly by doing painting and decorating jobs for a London garage chain. On 20 January 1977 Hart paid a visit in person to the garage company's offices in Hounslow, west London, to get his money.

The staff, already briefed by police that Hart was dangerous and wanted, delayed him long enough for the police to arrive. He went without a struggle to Richmond police station.

His first interview ended at 6.25 p.m. and he was returned to the cells. At 7.30 he was found near to death after attempting to hang himself from the cell door with his trouser belt. Although his breathing had stopped his life was saved.

Now Sewell and his team were more convinced than ever that they had their man. But, after four more days of interviews, Hart still vehemently denied being the killer.

Unexpected confession

Then, totally unexpectedly, Hart confessed. At 6.20 on the evening of 26 January Hart, who had his wife and brother-in-law with him in the interview room, suddenly gripped his wife's hand and said to detectives: "It was me, I shot the bank girl." ▶

2 THE GETAWAY: Hart returned the stolen car to the multi-storey car park. He picked up his own car to drive to his home in Basingstoke.

3 EVADING CAPTURE: Chased by police after another robbery, Hart escaped by taking to his heels across fields. A search of the abandoned car revealed a gun.

4 SHOTGUN SHELLS: A search of Hart's home uncovered stolen shotgun shells. But they appeared to be the wrong type.

But he insisted the shooting was an accident. He told Chief Superintendent Sewell: "I went to the bank and had the gun under my coat. I told her to give me the money. She was ages and ages. I banged on the glass with the gun and told her to hurry up. The money dropped into the tray. It was then the gun went off."

As detectives eagerly took down his every word, Hart explained how he had driven to Kingston in his own Wolseley car. At the multi-storey car park he had selected a maroon-coloured Austin A40 to steal to use as a getaway car.

After the shooting he had driven back to the car park and put the Austin back in the spot he had taken it from. He had then driven back to Basingstoke in his own car. It had broken down on the A3, and while all hell was breaking loose following the murder in Richmond, he had casually sat in his car waiting for the RAC to turn up to fix his motor.

Explaining in greater detail, he said that he had used a yellow raincoat he found in the Austin to cover up the gun as he walked into the bank, and had also worn a pair of tortoiseshell spectacles he had found in the car to complete his disguise.

Accidental shooting

Hart told detectives: "I used the dark wig and face make-up in the hope that people would think the job had been done by a Pakistani." He admitted that he had cocked both barrels of the near-antique weapon before going into the bank, but still insisted the shooting was an accident.

He said: "I did not mean to use it. I knew I had hit the girl because she screamed. I just hoped she was only wounded. I only found out she was dead when I heard about it on the TV."

The next day he took detectives to a garden where he had buried the sawn-off gun barrels. There was a fired cartridge in the

MICHAEL HART

Biography

Robbery with violence

Thirty-eight-year-old Michael Hart was a painter and decorator by trade. He was also a violent criminal, with numerous convictions for robbery and fraud. From his teens he had lived on the premise that hold-ups provided more money and less work than a regular job.

In the weeks prior to Angela's murder Hart had been arrested and charged with offences ranging from assault to car theft, burglary and robbery. He had appeared four times before magistrates at Basingstoke, and each time detectives had asked for him to be held in custody until his trail as they feared he may commit more offences. But their requests were turned down and he was granted bail. Hart, who was also wanted by police in Paris for the attemted murder of a French policeman, was ordered to report to the police every day as part of his bail conditions, which he did even on the day that he robbed Barclays Bank.

After being recognised during the attempted robbery at the garage, however, he went to ground in a caravan with a girlfriend.

Above: Michael Hart was a 38-year-old criminal wanted for a number of crimes, including a stabbing and a shooting.

Below: Hart was seen while making an attempted robbery at this Basingstoke service station.

right barrel and a live one in the left. Sure enough, the shells were part of the wrongly labelled batch stolen from the Reading gun shop. Police frogmen found the rest of the gun in the Thames near Hampton Court when Hart showed them the spot where he had thrown it in.

About this time Sewell's squad tracked down and brought in a 19-year-old woman friend of Hart, Sharon Stacey. The detectives were encouraged by her willingness to talk.

Stacey said that she had driven Hart to Kingston on the fateful day of Angela's murder. Tired of waiting to collect him, Sharon told the detectives that she had taken the train to get back to Basingstoke. At last, there was a witness to Hart's involvement.

But just as detectives were congratulating themselves on this apparently major break, she changed her mind, retracting her statement. She told police: "I was in a state and would have said anything. It was all lies."

Aware that Hart, too, might change his mind and retract his confession, Chief Superintendent Sewell wanted to get the forensic evidence in the bag as fast as possible.

Firearms specialist Brian Arnold assembled the gun, and his findings soon gave the

5 MANUFACTURER'S ERROR: *Analysis of the shells showed they had been wrongly labelled, and were of the type which had killed Angela.*

6 ARREST: *Hart was arrested while attempting to collect money for a decorating job. After questioning, he confessed to the bank shooting.*

7 RETRIEVING THE EVIDENCE: *Hart had dumped the murder weapon in the Thames. Police divers later recovered the shotgun from the spot indicated by Hart.*

Murder evidence

lie to Hart's claim that it had gone off accidentally. After making several successful test firings of the old-fashioned hammer gun, Arnold carried out pressure tests on the triggers.

He found that the one that had fired the deadly blast that took Angela's life needed six-and-a-half pounds pressure. The unfired trigger needed only three-and-a-half pounds pull. The gun expert tried various ways to make the gun go off accidentally, but found the only way was to slam the butt on the ground so hard that pieces chipped off it.

Glass fragments

The weapon had yet more secrets. More vital forensic evidence came from the unfired gun barrel in the shape of more than 1,000 microscopic fragments of glass from the screen that was designed to protect Angela.

The woman who owned the Austin used as a getaway car was traced. She told how she thought something odd had happened when she returned to the car and noticed it had been moved. An old raincoat, the one used by Hart to hide the gun, was missing. The same coat was dropped by the gunman at the bank.

The car also provided more damning scientific evidence to link Hart with the case. In it were scores more tiny glass shards from the bank screen which had been transferred to the vehicle via the gunman's clothing. Hart's Hampshire neighbours also reported seeing him burning things in his back garden shortly after the murder was reported. When police scientists sifted through his bonfire site they found the charred remains of the brown wig he had worn as a disguise.

One mystery has never been cleared up. Why did Michael Hart pull the trigger? One possibility seems to be that Angela, a strong-minded girl, might have infuriated Hart by being slow to hand over the money. Other officers who worked on the case believe Hart thought the shot would not penetrate the 'bulletproof' screen.

Guilty of murder

The trial opened at the Old Bailey on 3 November 1977, just a week short of a year since the murder. Despite the huge weight of forensic evidence against him, Hart refused to admit he had shot Angela in cold blood.

He did plead guilty to six counts of criminal deception and asked for another 39 cases to be taken into consideration.

The jury thought differently, however, and found Hart guilty of murder by a majority of 11 to 1. The judge, the Right Honourable Justice Melford Stevenson, gave him life imprisonment, with a recommendation that he should serve at least 25 years. □

Protective screen:
The glass over the teller's position in Barclays Bank was not thick enough to withstand a shotgun blast at very close range.

Shotgun cartridge:
When the shotgun was recovered from the Thames it contained one spent cartridge of the type which had been used to kill Angela Wooliscroft.

Automatic pistol:
The .22 automatic pistol found in the boot of the car Hart abandoned after a failed robbery attempt had been stolen, together with an ancient Reilly shotgun, from a gun shop in Reading.

Murder weapon:
Firearms experts were able to prove that both the gun and its ammunition were of the kind used in the robbery.

Shotgun barrels:
The shotgun was too long to be carried concealed, so Hart sawed the barrels off short and buried them in a garden. Police later recovered them.

Dark wig: Hart wore a dark wig and brown make-up during the robbery to confuse witnesses into thinking he was Asian. He also wore a pair of tortoiseshell sunglasses he had found in the stolen car.

Yellow raincoat:
Hart used a yellow raincoat to cover the shotgun as he entered the bank.

Below: Forensic analysis of the shot and shotgun used in the robbery at the bank was vital. It was this that proved decisive in the conviction of Michael Hart for the murder of Angela Wooliscroft.

HAROLD GREENWOOD

THE POISONED WINE

Welsh solicitor Harold Greenwood was far from being a pillar of society. Even so, he was not the kind of person one would expect to poison his wife with arsenic. But that is exactly what he was accused of doing.

Harold Greenwood was a respectable, if not greatly respected, member of the Carmarthenshire community. A solicitor with a practice in the town of Llanelli, Greenwood's property deals and involvement with money-lenders had earned him little professional credibility. He had few male friends, and had earned an unenviable reputation as a trouble-maker over his fondness for women. His salary was insufficient for the upkeep of the family's Kidwelly home, Rumsey House, a rambling three-storey stone mansion, and the shortfall was met from Mrs Greenwood's modest private income. Nevertheless, the Greenwoods were regarded as a reasonably harmonious couple.

Lunch at Kidwelly on Sunday 15 June 1919 consisted of a joint of meat and vegetables, followed by gooseberry tart and custard. Greenwood drank whisky; the two children, Irene and Kenneth, drank water; and Mrs Greenwood had a couple of glasses of Burgundy.

The only unusual feature of the meal was that the maid, Hannah Williams, had been hindered in laying the table because Greenwood had been bustling about in the china pantry, a room just off the kitchen, between 12.30 and 1 p.m. Greenwood later claimed that he frequently used the pantry sink to wash his hands, although Hannah had never known him to do it before.

After lunch, Mabel Greenwood took a walk in the garden. She was 47 and not in the best of health, never having really recovered from giving birth to their younger child 10 years earlier. She had a weak heart and a small tumour, and often voiced her fear of cancer. Indeed, her husband had confided to friends that Mabel had been complaining of pains which prevented her sleeping; he even went so far as to suggest that she might not be long for this world.

Mabel falls ill

Between 6.30 and 7 p.m. that evening, Mrs Greenwood complained of sickness and suffocating pains around her heart. Greenwood gave her brandy. At 7 p.m. he went across the road to summon the family doctor, Dr Thomas Griffiths, who found his patient sitting on a couch vomiting. Young Irene sent her mother to bed when she developed diarrhoea. Meanwhile, Greenwood and the doctor took their minds off Mrs Greenwood's suffering by playing a few rounds of clock-golf in the garden.

Back in the house, a Miss Phillips, who

In July 1896 Harold Greenwood married Mabel Vansittart Bowater. Mabel's family was wealthy – her brother, Sir Thomas Vansittart Bowater, became the Lord Mayor of London in 1913. Her private income enabled the family to live in style.

Left: Harold Greenwood, seen here in his study, had a somewhat dubious reputation in his hometown of Kidwelly, a few miles west along the coast of Carmarthen Bay. The family home (main picture above) cost considerably more than he could afford on his salary, but fortunately his wife had a private income.

had called round about a supper invitation, was alarmed to find her hostess so poorly and sent for the district nurse.

Nurse Jones arrived, but Mrs Greenwood's condition steadily worsened. She was given brandy, milk and soda, but could not keep anything down. By 1 a.m. the patient seemed to realise the seriousness of her condition and was heard in prayer.

Dr Griffiths was summoned four more times during the night, although he

Less than a month after Mabel's death, Harold Greenwood became engaged to Gladys Jones, and they got married three months later. Had he killed his first wife to make room for the second? Or was he simply an amiable, happy-go-lucky ladies' man who foolishly married again without thinking what gossiping tongues would say?

▶ explained Mrs Greenwood's suffering as nothing more than a touch of gastric trouble, probably brought on by the gooseberry tart. Greenwood himself was no less casual in his approach. On one occasion he took so long fetching the doctor that his daughter had to go to see what had become of him.

In all the toing and froing between the surgery and his home, Greenwood found the opportunity to spend what some might call an indiscreet amount of time with the doctor's sister, Miss Mary Griffiths, to whom he had been paying attention for some time. On this particular night, Harold

Below: Greenwood is ushered into the Carmarthen Guildhall. Local feeling in Llanelli was strongly against the wayward solicitor. However, being tried in the county town 12 miles away worked in Greenwood's favour, since Carmarthen juries were notorious for their reluctance to convict.

Below: Harold Greenwood leaves Carmarthen Prison in a closed carriage. An eager crowd lined the short distance to the Assizes, which were being held in the Guildhall only 100 yards from the jail, hoping for a glimpse of the accused.

Daily Mirror masthead and photographs:

OR ABSENT TO SEND CENOTAPH WREATHS

The Daily Mirror

CIRCULATION LARGER THAN THAT OF ANY OTHER DAILY PICTURE PAPER

WEDNESDAY, NOVEMBER 3, 1920 [16 PAGES] One Penny.

SIVE OPENING OF THE GREENWOOD TRIAL

Mrs. Gladys Greenwood (nearest camera), the second wife of the prisoner, walking with a friend at Carmarthen. She has paid frequent visits to her husband.

Daily Mirror photograph of Mr. Harold Greenwood. He pleaded not guilty.

Dr. Griffiths, medical attendant to the late Mrs. Greenwood, yesterday corrected his evidence regarding morphia in pills.

Sir E. Marlay Samson outlined the case for the prosecution in slow, reserved tones.

Mr. Justice Shearman arriving at the court. The trial is taking place in the Shire Hall, Carmarthen.

Left: At the beginning of the century, trials were a popular form of entertainment. Although the Greenwood case was a small provincial affair, it still made headlines in the London press, and filled the entire front page of the Daily Mirror.

informed Miss Griffiths that a fortune-teller had recently told him to look forward to a honeymoon shortly – which he mentioned cheerfully despite the fact that his wife of 23 years was seriously ill.

Fatal coma

At just after 1 a.m., Mabel Greenwood was given some pills prescribed by Dr Griffiths and fetched from his surgery by Greenwood. She immediately fell into a coma from which she never recovered, and by 3.30 a.m. her suffering was over. Dr Griffiths certified the cause of death as valvular disease of the heart.

Harold Greenwood's behaviour following his wife's death was hardly that of the grieving widower. On the very morning that Mabel died, Greenwood visited Miss Gladys Jones, the sister of one of his friends; he borrowed £20 from her, and then took her on a shopping expedition to buy his mourning clothes.

Within a month Greenwood was shopping again – this time for a £55 diamond cluster ring for Miss Jones. The fortune-teller had been right: four months after Mabel's death, Gladys became the second Mrs Greenwood, to almost universal scandal and dismay. If the circumstances surrounding Mabel Greenwood's death had not seemed quite right at the time, then surely this hasty marriage would galvanise suspicion into accusation.

When he returned from his honeymoon, Greenwood was interviewed by Police Superintendent Jones, for the first time on 24 October and again on the 31st. He was informed that with regard to certain rumours, the police were applying for an exhumation order on Mrs Greenwood's body.

Post-mortem examination

The post-mortem examination of Mabel Greenwood's remains, which were very well preserved, took place in Kidwelly Town Hall on 16 April 1920. The report by Mr Webster, official analyst to the Home Office, was presented to the inquest on Mrs Greenwood. At this time the coroner's courts were empowered not only to bring in a verdict on the cause of death, but to comment on how that cause had been effected and who had 'effected' it.

On 16 June 1920, the first anniversary of Mrs Greenwood's death, Mr George

The Trial

Did Mabel Greenwood die by accident?

Greenwood's defence proposed that Mabel may have been given the poison by accident. They said that she could have been prescribed the wrong pills at the time of her illness.

But the suggestion that Dr Griffiths might have confused a bottle of bismuth pills for its neighbour on the shelf containing Fowler's solution of arsenic was ruled out.

Poor medical evidence

Even so, the doctor, by now retired, made a poor showing in court. Sir Edward Marshall Hall was prepared to show that Mrs Greenwood had died from morphia poisoning, as the result of Dr Griffiths mistakenly administering a lethal dose of half a grain of that drug.

To the prosecution's consternation, Griffiths let slip that he was in the habit of using the term morphia when he really meant opium. Half a grain of opium would have eased Mabel's discomfort. But half a grain of morphia, which is 20 times as strong, would have been fatal.

Harold Greenwood listens intently to his defence counsel, Sir Edward Marshall Hall, as he casts doubt on the medical evidence against the solicitor.

Jones, foreman of the jury, handed the coroner this note: "We are unanimously of the opinion that the death of the deceased, Mabel Greenwood, was caused by arsenical poisoning . . . and that the poison was administered by Harold Greenwood." The public gallery erupted in delighted applause.

On trial for murder

Greenwood duly went on trial at Carmarthen Assizes, where his case was heard before Mr Justice Shearman. Sir Edward Marshall Hall KC defended Greenwood, and Sir Edward Marlay Samson led the prosecution case for the Crown. He said that the defendant had deliberately contaminated Mrs Greenwood's lunchtime Burgundy with sufficient weedkiller to cause "death in one glass".

The court was told that Harold Greenwood had bought tins of a brand of weedkiller called 'Eureka' in February and April 1919. This was a compound of sodium arsenate in the form of an easily soluble pink powder: the weedkiller would only very slightly darken the colour of red wine, and there would be no discernible taste. Eureka contained about 55 per cent

arsenic, and at this concentration four grains would be fatal. Forty grains, or half a teaspoonful, would need to be added to a bottle of wine to achieve the minimum fatal dose of about two grains of arsenic in each glass.

Dr William Willcox, consulting medical adviser to the Home Office, presented the medical evidence, stating that a total of 18 milligrams, or 0.28 grains, of arsenic was found in Mabel Greenwood's body. The amount found in the gullet, stomach, intestines and rectum was 6.1 milligrams, indicating that the poison was taken orally. The wide distribution of the poison suggested that it was taken several hours before death, and almost certainly in a dissolved rather than a solid state; the absence of visible solid particles in the viscera bore this out.

The fact that so little of the arsenic was found in the stomach indicated that none was ingested in the three hours before death. The poison, Willcox concluded, would most likely have been administered between 1.30 and 6.30 in the afternoon, with severe vomiting and diarrhoea leading to heart failure and collapse, and death resulting within 10 hours of the onset of illness.

Mrs Greenwood's reported symptoms conformed to those of arsenic poisoning. The presence of arsenic in the body was indisputable, but how did it get there? Suicide was ruled out from the start.

The defence then proposed a number of not entirely convincing alternatives. It could, they said, have been taken accidentally; the gooseberries might have been sprayed with an arsenic-based weedkiller – but then all the family would have shown symptoms. Atmospheric vapour

The case against Greenwood hinged on two main points. Mabel Greenwood had undoubtedly been poisoned, but was it arsenic that had killed her? And, if so, could it have been administered by accident.

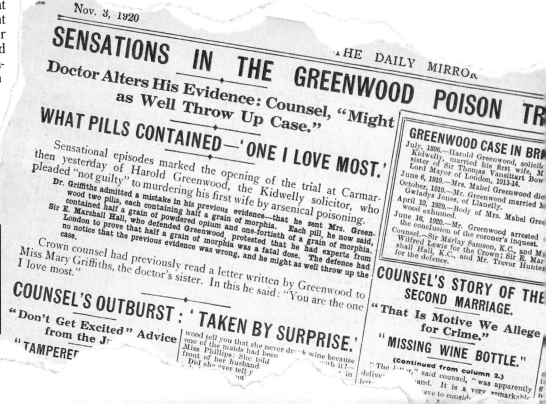

Nov. 3, 1920

SENSATIONS IN THE GREENWOOD POISON TR

Doctor Alters His Evidence: Counsel, "Might as Well Throw Up Case."

WHAT PILLS CONTAINED – 'ONE I LOVE MOST.'

Sensational episodes marked the opening of the trial at Carmarthen yesterday of Harold Greenwood, the Kidwelly solicitor, who pleaded "not guilty" to murdering his first wife by arsenical poisoning.

Dr. Griffiths admitted a mistake in his previous evidence—that he sent Mrs. Greenwood two pills, each containing half a grain of morphia. Each pill, he now said, contained half a grain of powdered opium and one-fortieth of a grain of morphia. Sir E. Marshall Hall, who defended Greenwood, protested that half a grain of morphia was a fatal dose. The defence had London to prove that half a grain of morphia was wrong, and he might as well throw up the no notice that the previous evidence was wrong, and he might as well throw up the case.

Crown counsel had previously read a letter written by Greenwood to Miss Mary Griffiths, the doctor's sister. In this he said: "You are the one I love most."

COUNSEL'S OUTBURST : 'TAKEN BY SURPRISE.'

"Don't Get Excited" Advice from the Ju...

"TAMPERE...

...wood tell you that she never dr...k wine because one of the maids had been...
Miss Phillips: She told...
front of her husband...
Did she ever tell y...

GREENWOOD CASE IN BR...

July, 1896.—Harold Greenwood, solicit...
Kidwelly, married his first wife, M...
sister of Sir Thomas Vansittart Bow...
Lord Mayor of London, 1913-14.
June 6, 1919.—Mrs. Mabel Greenwood die...
October, 1919.—Mr. Greenwood married M...
Gwladys Jones, of Llanelly.
April 10, 1920.—Body of Mrs. Mabel Gree...
wood exhumed.
June 16, 1920.—Mr. Greenwood arrested...
the conclusion of the coroner's inquest.
Counsel—Sir Marlay Samson, K.C., and...
Wilfred Lewis for the Crown; Sir E. Mar...
shall Hall, K.C., and Mr. Trevor Hunter...
for the defence.

COUNSEL'S STORY OF THE SECOND MARRIAGE.

"That Is Motive We Allege for Crime."

"MISSING WINE BOTTLE."

(Continued from column 2.)

"The l...," said counsel, "was apparently...
delive...and. It is a very remarkable...
lett...ave to consid...

from the weedkiller in the garden might have been inhaled – but, if so, why had Greenwood and the doctor not been affected when they were playing golf? Or perhaps Mrs Greenwood could have taken it by mistake. She was known to use patent medicines, some of which contained arsenic, and so arsenic would have been found in her body, whatever the cause of death.

Was it gastroenteritis?

And so the defence began to turn on the hypothesis that the arsenic in the body was less than a fatal dose – or at any rate incidental to the cause of death. Certainly it has been known for a living body to contain two-and-a-half grains of arsenic with no ill effect; could Mabel Greenwood have merely suffered a gastric attack, to which she was prone, provoked by the gooseberries? Her symptoms were, by and large, the same as those of gastroenteritis.

There was also some last-minute evidence from Greenwood's daughter Irene, who swore on oath that she too had drunk

Irene Greenwood's testimony was vital to her father's defence. Irene (seen here in the centre) stated that she too had drunk from the bottle of Burgundy which had supposedly contained the fatal dose of poison at lunchtime and at supper, and had suffered no ill effects. The testimony of a visitor who saw no wine on the table at supper apparently did not convince the jury.

Harold Greenwood leaves court after his acquittal with his new wife, Gladys. The notoriety aroused by the case meant that Greenwood could no longer make a living in Llanelli, and the couple were forced to move to England. Greenwood died in 1929 in a village in Hertfordshire.

wine at lunch and supper, from the same bottle. But Miss Phillips, who visited the house later, swore there was no wine at all on the supper table.

The prosecution found it hard to establish what motive Greenwood might have had for killing his wife. Her life was not insured, and her private income of £600 per year would be lost on her death. His new wife Gladys Jones was without capital or prospects, and there was no reason to kill his wife in order to have an affair: Greenwood had been doing that anyway, with more than one woman.

Swayed by the eloquence of Marshall Hall and despite the unlikeliness of some of the defence theories, the jury returned a verdict of not guilty.

However, in a note not published at the time, they did voice a substantial doubt. In it they expressed their opinion that a dangerous dose of arsenic had been administered, but that it was not the indisputable cause of death: "The evidence before us is insufficient, and does not conclusively satisfy us as to how, and by whom, the arsenic was administered."

Death announcement

Less than nine years after the trial, a few paragraphs in the newspaper announced the death on 17 January 1929 in a remote Hertfordshire village of a man who had lived there dogged by poverty, ill-health and notoriety. It was Harold Greenwood, living under the assumed name of 'Pilkington'.

Greenwood was buried in an unmarked grave in Llanelli, not far from Mabel. His second wife, Gladys, returned to live in South Wales, where she remained until her death in the 1950s.

Shotgun Suicide?

At first glance it was an open and shut case. The body was on the bed, a huge hole blown through its face. On the floor lay a shotgun. It looked like suicide – but was it?

The body lay on its back on the bed. Blood shone obscenely in the light, from a hole which had been punched through the head: a fist-sized hole, right between the eyes. It was not a pretty sight. Still, the uniformed police who were first on the scene were used to such sights. After all, this was Miami, and Miami could be a rough city.

Monday 8 September 1986 had just begun. The long Miami weekend was drawing to a close, and the operators manning the lines of Miami's '911' emergency telephone service had had a typically busy time, but the rush was now over.

"Jack's been shot!"

The call came in just before one in the morning. It was a tragically routine affair in the crime-ridden Florida metropolis. A distraught female voice had cried "Jack's been shot!"

Police were sent to Number 80, North West 69th Avenue. The house was in a poor- to middle-class area of Miami, a part of the city where violent crime was not unusual.

First on the scene were the uniformed officers, dispatched on receipt of the 911 call, who arrived at the house within minutes. They were soon joined by detectives from the Miami City Police's homicide department and the duty Medical Examiner from Metro-Dade County, who is called in on any occasion of violent death.

The house was a low, one-storey building. On entering, the first thing the investigators noticed was the unusual decor. There were fur rugs everywhere, and on the walls there was a collection of native spears. The bedroom, on the south side of the house, was dominated by a large, fur-covered water-bed. A lamp with a Harley-Davidson

Right: Everything about Jack Sebastian said 'biker', from the Harley-Davidson memorabilia scattered about the house to the extensive tattoos with which he had decorated his body.

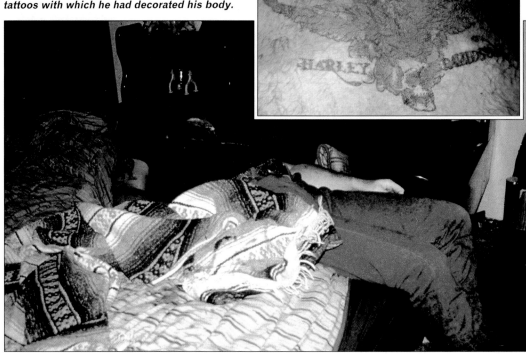

Above: The scene that greeted investigators at Number N0, North West 69th Avenue was gruesome. The body of Jack Sebastian was sprawled over the bed, his brains blown out by a shotgun.

shade lit the scene.

Lying on its back across the bed, partly covered by a quilt and Indian-style blanket, was a man's body. The body was black-haired and heavily bearded. One blue eye gleamed in the light; the other eye had been obliterated, and most of the left side of the face was covered in blood.

Unusual decor

The dead man was pretty big – just under six feet tall and heavily built. He was dressed like a

On the floor of the bedroom, right by the feet of the body, lay a 12-gauge Smith & Wesson Model 916 pump-action shotgun. This was almost certainly the fatal weapon, but that would require forensic confirmation.

The pattern of gunshot

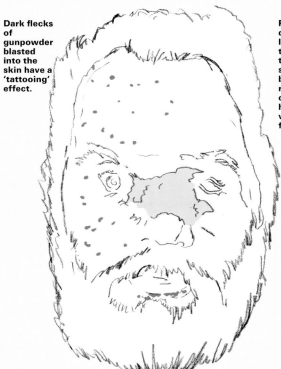

Dark flecks of gunpowder blasted into the skin have a 'tattooing' effect.

From a distance of less than two feet the shotgun blast ripped a 7 cm × 4 cm hole in the victim's face.

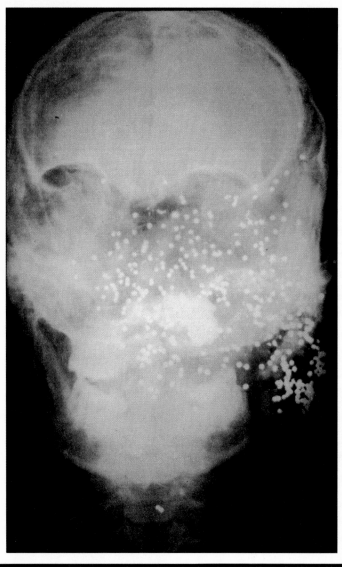

The most obvious injury to the body was the huge hole caused by the shotgun blast. Lead shot spraying out within the left side of the skull was visible on the X-ray. However, there was also a giveaway 'stippling' of the skin, where flecks of gunpowder had been blasted into the face.

Above: Shotguns are ferocious weapons at close range. The densely-packed slugs from the cartridge blast a huge entry wound, much bigger than that caused by a bullet.

Right: A head X-ray shows a pattern of slugs below and to the left-hand side of the victim's face. The fatal shot must, therefore, have come from above and to his right.

---

biker, in a black T-shirt, blue jeans, black boots and a snake-skin belt. A photo of the man mounted on a Harley-Davidson lay on the bedside table next to some empty plastic bags that had possibly contained cocaine. A roach clip – a device to hold a marijuana 'joint' so that it can be smoked right down to the end – was also on the table.

On the floor behind the door, only a few inches away from the body's booted feet, lay a Smith & Wesson pump-action shotgun – it had been fired once.

The dead man's name was Jack Sebastian, and it was his girlfriend, Diane Shelton, who had called the police. Now she began to tell the investigating officers what had happened.

Homicide connection

Marginally involved in Miami's drugs trade, Sebastian had been named in connection with a recent homicide. He was free on bail for the moment, but with a

court case hanging over his head he had become very depressed.

The couple had been out drinking at the nearby Pine Tree Lounge, and had an argument. According to Diane, Jack had threatened suicide, and he had left the bar while she was in the bathroom. She had stayed and had a lot to drink.

Girlfriend's story

On returning to the house, Diane claimed that she had found Sebastian sitting on the bed holding a shotgun. He said that he was going to kill himself, and fired one shot.

At first glance the scene did indeed look like a suicide, and the first police reports tentatively came to that conclusion. But Lyvia A. Alvarez, the Medical Examiner on the scene, had her

The table by Jack Sebastian's bed revealed a lot about the man. It was cluttered with personal items, many being motorbike- or drug-related.

doubts. Most gun suicides are carried out with the muzzle of the gun in contact with the skin.

In this case, however, there was a massive entry wound between the eyes, which was larger than would have been expected with a contact shot. Additionally, there was extensive

'stippling' – small black powder marks – all over the forehead, nose and stretching down as far as the lower lip.

Shotguns fire a cloud of lead shot, which expands the further it flies from the muzzle. The extent of marking on Jack Sebastian's face indicated that the ▶

Test-firing for shot pattern

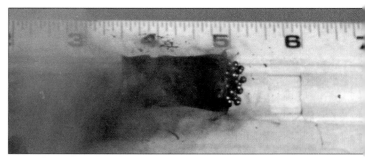

Ballistics experts carried out a series of tests on the shotgun. High-speed cameras, flash and film were used to stop the action of the cartridge in flight at a number of distances from the muzzle (above). They also fired the weapon at a white card from various distances (right). The resultant shot pattern was measured and compared to that on the victim's face.

Above: Milliseconds after firing, within two inches of the muzzle, shotgun pellets stay in a solid mass, held together by the cartridge case.

Above: By the time the slug has travelled five inches, the packing begins to be ripped off by air pressure, allowing the pellets to start spreading.

▶ muzzle of the shotgun had been some distance from the skin when it was fired. This conclusion was enough for the police to change their findings from suicide to possible homicide, pending autopsy and ballistic reports.

Was it murder?

The body was removed to the Metro-Dade County Medical Examiner's Department, where Dr Alvarez conducted the post-mortem examination the following morning. The cause of death was obviously the gunshot wound to the head. The path of the wound was from right to left, and downwards. In other words, the weapon had been fired from above the victim's head and to the right. The investigators thought it was extremely unlikely that a suicide would hold a long weapon like a shotgun above his head and to one side – another pointer towards murder.

Ballistic tests

The next stage was to examine the shotgun taken from the scene and the fired shotgun shell in its chamber. The gun was a standard Smith & Wesson Model 916 pump-action weapon; it had had its serial number obliterated, indicating that it had been illegally acquired.

The Metro-Dade Crime Laboratory first fired a shell through the shotgun, and then the ballistics experts made a microscopic comparison with the case found in the gun at the scene. They confirmed that both had been fired from the same gun.

Above: Criminalist Ray Freeman of the Metro-Dade Police Department Crime Lab Bureau shoots at a white card to test the dispersal of shot.

The ballistics experts then tested the performance of the gun. Several rounds were fired and the spread of shot was measured at various distances. The findings indicated that the fatal shot had been fired with the shotgun's muzzle between 18 inches and two feet away from Jack Sebastian's head.

The next step was to check whether Sebastian's arms could stretch far enough to reach the trigger of the shotgun. Tests conducted with the body showed that they were, but only if the muzzle was positioned right up against the face.

By shooting at the card from various distances, the forensic scientists were able to compare their results with the wound on Jack Sebastian's face. The shot fired from two feet (No. 2 on the card) was the closest match.

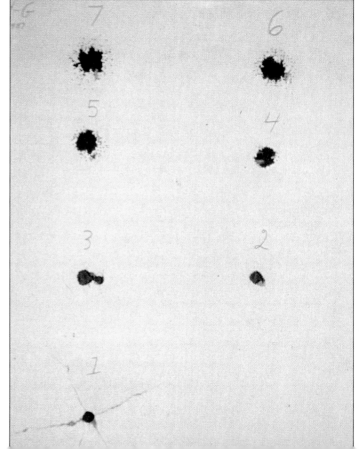

Above: At 20 inches from the muzzle, the lead shot is almost free of the packaging, and the wadding at the base has separated completely.

It was just possible for a big man to commit suicide and get the required muzzle clearance, but only by holding the gun between his legs and triggering the weapon with his toes. But if fired in that way the shot would have entered the head from below. In any case, Sebastian had been wearing boots when found, and he could not have pulled the trigger. If it could not have been suicide, then it had to be murder.

Obvious suspect

Diane Shelton was the obvious suspect. She had already admitted to arguing with her boyfriend, and her original suicide story was a lie. Presented with incontrovertible scientific proof, she admitted to killing her lover.

On the night in question she had gone back to Sebastian's

Above: After 24 inches, the shot starts spreading out, and wounds created beyond this distance are significantly increased in size.

house. Very much the worse for drink, she was angry at being left in the Pine Tree Lounge. The argument which had started in the bar continued, and she threatened him with the shotgun. One shot, and Jack Sebastian was dead.

Diane Shelton was tried in October 1987, accused of second-degree murder. In her defence she claimed that she had been drunk and had not known that the weapon was loaded. Nevertheless, she was convicted and sentenced to a long term of imprisonment.

Too far for suicide

In addition to the ballistic evidence, the forensic examiners also tested physical evidence. Could the victim have fired the gun from the angle indicated by the wound? Tests by crime laboratory personnel using the body showed that it would only be possible with the muzzle close to the head. But shot pattern analysis showed that the muzzle of the shotgun must have been at least 18 inches from the face when it was fired. This inconsistency completely ruled out suicide; it had to be murder.

Right: The spread of shot shown by the outer circle on the X-ray proved that the gun had been fired some distance from the victim's face.

Below: Investigators re-enact the angle from which the gun was fired to produce the wounds shown on the X-ray. They then used the corpse (inset) to confirm that suicide was impossible.

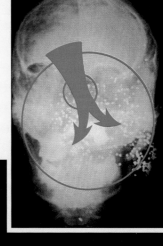

BODKIN ADAMS

MURDERER or mercy killer?

It was one of the most sensational cases of the 1950s. A portly doctor, a pillar of south coast society, was accused of murdering his patients for their inheritances.

During the summer of 1956 the south-coast resort of Eastbourne was abuzz with rumours that a "mass murderer" was living in the town. The locals whispered and the press ran stories about the "Bluebeard" who specialised in poisoning wealthy women. Slowly the finger began to point to John Bodkin Adams, a 58-year-old local doctor.

To many locals Dr Adams was nothing more than an upright, God-fearing medical man: a man who was a churchwarden, who taught Sunday school and who was chairman of the local YMCA. But to many others the rumours confirmed what they had always suspected – that the portly, balding Adams was greedy and grasping, a man quite capable of giving a patient an overdose for financial gain. For time and again they had seen his name among the beneficiaries in the published wills of his dead patients. And they had seen both him and his practice become affluent. But most importantly he had arranged to have several patients cremated rather than buried. Many suspected that this was to burn the evidence that he had poisoned them!

Above: Ulster-born Dr John Bodkin Adams was a short, portly man who came from a family of doctors. Arriving in Eastbourne in the 1920s, he quickly established a highly successful and prosperous practice catering to the needs of the wealthy end of local society.

Left: 'Bobbie' Hullet was a wealthy socialite whose death while under Adams' treatment led to a police investigation and murder charges.

Right: The body of Mrs Julia Bradnum, who died in 1952 aged 85, was exhumed four years later. Adams was her doctor when she died and she had left him £800 in her will.

Experienced doctor

Dr Adams, a bachelor cared for by a devoted housekeeper, had been in private practice in the town for 35 years. Born in Northern Ireland in 1899, he was raised by his widowed mother (his father had died during World War I), a temperance campaigner who had made her son sign the pledge when he was nine.

He qualified as a doctor in Belfast and, at the age of 23, successfully answered an advert in a religious periodical for 'a Christian young doctor-assistant with a view to partnership'. He bought a house in Eastbourne and brought his mother from Ulster to live with him. He began to visit his patients by motorcycle. This was replaced by a two-seater car, then a saloon, and finally a chauffeur-driven car. By the mid-1930s he had 2,000 patients, half of

them private, half 'panel' paying sixpence or a shilling a week. From time to time he was left legacies by grateful patients; one, by a Mrs Whitton in 1935, was for the princely sum of £3,000.

Dr Adams had signed her death certificate ('myocardial degeneration and high blood pressure'). He was also named as executor of her will, which the family were to contest without success.

That was when tongues began to wag. For soon after, Adams received a postcard on which was scrawled: "Keep your fingers crossed and don't bump off any more wealthy widows." He tore it up. But he could not so easily stem the whispering campaign which persisted for the next 20 years.

It was the apparent suicide in July 1956 of another of his patients, Mrs Gertrude

'Bobbie' Hullet, that sealed Adams' fate. He wrote to tell the coroner that he had administered strictly controlled doses of sleeping pills, but that she "could not possibly have secreted any of this"; and he had searched the room for empty bottles or cartons, but found "nothing to suggest poison".

Was it murder?

What made his situation worse in the eyes of the police and coroner was that Mrs Hullet had given Adams £1,000 to buy himself a new car. They had seriously to consider murder. The coroner ordered a second post-mortem. It was performed by Professor Francis Camps, the Home Office pathologist whose very name was synonymous with murder investigations.

At the inquest on Mrs Hullet's death Camps said he had found a fatal dose of 115 grains (about 20 tablets) of the sleeping drug sodium barbitone in her body. The verdict was suicide. That effectively cleared Adams of 'foul play'. But he was very definitely not in the clear so far as the press and police were concerned.

Suspected poisonings

On 22 August 1956 the *Daily Mail*'s headline read: 'Yard probe mass poisoning. 25 deaths in the great mystery of Eastbourne.' And later: 'Enquiry into 400 wills: rich women believed to have been the victims.' The paper revealed that Scotland Yard's murder squad was 'investigating the suspected mass poisoning of wealthy women in Eastbourne during the past 20 years.' The foreign press, not bound by British libel law, went one step further: 'is the Bluebeard of Eastbourne about to be unmasked?'

Police turned their attention to Mrs Edith Morrell, a former Adams patient who died six years earlier, aged 81. Everything seemed to fit a murder theory. Adams had

been left a Rolls-Royce and a chest of silver.

Also, when he had filled in the form for Mrs Morrell's cremation, Adams had stated that he was "not aware of" any pecuniary interest in her death, yet just before she died he had visited her solicitor to say that she had forgotten to add a codicil to her will leaving him her Rolls-Royce and the contents of a jewellery case. He maintained that although she was very ill, she was fit enough to execute the codicil. Finally, during the two years Adams had treated her for hardening of the arteries, she had suffered a stroke that had paralysed her left side. Nurses said she was seldom in pain. Yet Adams had repeatedly prescribed large doses of pain-killing drugs.

On 26 November Adams called at Police HQ where he was told by the officer in charge of the investigation, Detective Superintendent Hannam, that he was still making enquiries into "the deaths of some of your rich patients". Adams asked which. Hannam replied that Mrs Morrell was one. Adams replied: "Easing the passing of a dying patient is not all that wicked. She wanted to die. That cannot be murder."

Two local newsmen talked to the Chief Constable but he told them little. However, as they left an officer in an outer office said: "You on this Hullet job? Well, it's about time somebody caught up with that bloody doctor."

The newsmen's tip-off to Fleet Street brought a posse of reporters to Eastbourne. The Chief Constable told them that there was a "possibility of foul play" in Mrs Hullet's death. The headline in the *Daily Sketch* the following morning read: "Was the £1,000 widow murdered?" It virtually named Adams as the killer.

The inheritor

Between 1944 and 1955 Dr Bodkin Adams received 14 bequests from among his many elderly patients – bequests that fuelled the flames of the 'Bluebeard' rumour:

£1,000 from Mrs Irene Herbert (who left £11,000)
£4,000 in shares from Mrs Emily Mortimer (£15,000)
£1,000 from Mrs Amy I'Anson Ware (£9,000)
Rolls-Royce car and silver cutlery from Mrs Edith Morrell (£175,000)
£200 and a clock from Mrs Annabella Kilgour (£53,000)
£100 from Mrs Mary Prince (£5,000)
£1,000 from Mrs Gertrude Hullet (£17,000)
£800 from Mrs Julia Bradnum (£4,000)
£500 from Mrs Annie Dowding (£11,000)
£5,200 from Miss Clara Miller (£7,000)
£750 from Miss Florence Cavill (£7,000)
£100 from Mr Sidney Prince (£91,000)
£250 from Mr George Blunt (£18,000)
£1,000 from Mr James Downs (£27,000)

Edith Morrell, who died aged 81 in 1950, was one of the wealthiest of Adams' patient/benefactors.

Bodkin at bay: did he kill his patients?

It was on 24 November 1956 that police went to Dr Adams' home with a Dangerous Drugs Act search warrant; while his house was being searched, he was quizzed about his medical treatment of Mrs Morrell. The next day Adams was taken to Police HQ in Eastbourne, where 13 charges (mainly minor offences concerning National Health prescriptions and false declarations under the Cremation Act, 1902) were laid against him.

Left: Once the press got hold of the story of a killer doctor in Eastbourne, it was not long before they had tracked Dr Bodkin Adams down and photographers began hounding him.

He was released on police bail; he and his solicitor, Mr H.V. James, drove back to Adams' house. It was the Cremation Act charges in relation to four of Adams' former patients that worried the solicitor. He made Adams go over everything that police had said to him when they had searched his house. Adams said that most of their questions had centred around Mrs Morrell.

Medical records

Because of all the speculation in the press about a 'mass poisoner', James feared that it would not be long before police would make their next move. So, did Adams have any records of Mrs Morrell's medical treatment?

Adams recalled having been sent the nurses' written records in a parcel shortly after her death, but couldn't remember what had happened to them – and thought it very unlikely that he still had them. Fortunately for Adams, the solicitor decided to search the house, room by room, cupboard by cupboard.

At 3 a.m. he was rewarded – there, at the back of a drawer, was a brown-paper parcel containing eight notebooks. In them were the hour-by-hour handwritten records of the four nurses who had looked after Mrs Morrell from 1 June 1949 to her death on 13 November 1950. The following month Adams was charged with murder.

Browne's chemist shop in Eastbourne provided details of prescriptions written by Bodkin Adams in 1950 when he was treating Mrs Morrell.

On 19 December Hannam made his move and arrested Adams at his home. Adams said: "Murder? Can you prove it was murder?" Hannam formally charged Adams with the murder of Mrs Morrell. Adams added: "I did not think you could prove murder. She was dying in any event."

The Crown prosecution were to make full use of Adams' reply when his trial opened at the Old Bailey on 18 March 1957, before Mr Justice Patrick Devlin.

The Attorney-General, Sir Reginald Manningham-Buller, drew the jury's attention to the words, "I did not think you could prove murder" and asked: "Is that what you would expect an innocent man to say when he is charged with murder, or is it what a man might say if he committed a murder, but thought he had done it so cleverly that his guilt could not be proved?"

The testimonies of the four nurses who had attended Mrs Morrell demonstrated that Adams gave "unusually large amounts of drugs" even when Mrs Morrell was in a coma. "Why," he asked, "were those large injections given to an unconscious woman on the doctor's orders?"

He went on to submit that if Mrs Morrell was a dying woman when the injections were given, then she was dying from over-

doses of morphia and heroin which the doctor had prescribed.

But the nurses were relying on memory from seven years earlier, and when cross-examined by defending counsel, Sir Geoffrey Lawrence, the case for the Crown began to go badly wrong. Lawrence produced the nurses' original written records, in notebook form, from June 1949 to November 1950. These showed that far from being comatose from drugs, Mrs Morrell had a good appetite, drank brandy and soda, and once told a nurse who had not answered a bedside bell that she was "a nasty, common woman!"

Nurses' evidence

Nurse Stronach had testified that Mrs Morrell was "rambling and semi-conscious", but the notebooks showed that on that day she had lunch of partridge, celery, pudding, and brandy and soda. Nurse Stronach also said that Mrs Morrell was dopey and half-asleep when Adams gave her the night injection because she, Nurse Stronach, had already given one. But Nurse Stronach's handwritten notes showed she had *not* given an injection; her memory, she had to admit, was at fault.

The notebooks also revealed that Sister

Mason-Ellis had given Mrs Morrell a *standard* injection of painkiller (¼ grain of morphia, ½ grain of heroin) nightly, month after month. And that far from being heavily sedated days before her death, Mrs Morrell had a hearty appetite.

Then Nurse Randall's notes revealed that in September 1950, Adams had holidayed in Scotland; and that Dr Harris, his partner, had continued treating Mrs Morrell with the *same* drugs that Adams had prescribed.

On the night Mrs Morrell died Nurse Randall's notes showed that Adams had injected Mrs Morrell with 5 c.c. of paraldehyde to help her sleep (which the prosecution alleged was the overdose that killed her). The nurse believed 5 c.c. was "a very large dose" and that 2 c.c. was normal. Lawrence then asked Nurse Randall if she knew that a British Pharmacopoeia *full* dose of paraldehyde was 8 c.c. The nurse admitted that she did not.

Not guilty of murder

The catalogue of contradictions between the nurses' testimonies from memory and what was written in their original notebooks seriously undermined the prosecution's case against Adams. And though the trial was to go on for a further 12 days, the murder charge was effectively lost.

The jury of 10 men and two women took 44 minutes to reach a not guilty verdict. Dr Adams was later fined £2,400 for minor offences on the original indictment and struck off the Medical Register. He was reinstated in 1961. He died in 1983, aged 84, after a fall while clay-pigeon shooting.

Mrs Morrell's nurses were key witnesses, but their memories proved to be less reliable than the notes made at the time.

Above: The massive publicity surrounding the trial meant that spectators began queuing before dawn in order to get a seat in court.

Right: Thanks to his own records and the poor quality of evidence presented by the prosecution, Adams was acquitted of murder. He was later found guilty of a number of less serious offences and was struck off the Medical Register.

Four years after the trial Bodkin Adams was once again a doctor. While he was never fully accepted back into society, Adams continued to live life to the full. He died in 1983, after an accident while shooting in Sussex. Ironically, among the many small bequests in his will, he left a small sum for his own doctor.

57

KIDNAPPED AND BRAINWASHED

Patricia Hearst, heiress to one of the biggest fortunes in America, was snatched from her apartment by a sinister terrorist group.

O n 4 February 1974 Patricia Campbell Hearst, 19-year-old daughter of American newspaper tycoon Randolph Hearst, was taking a shower in the San Francisco apartment she shared with her boyfriend, Steven Weed. Suddenly and without warning a white woman and two black men broke into the flat, and in the struggle that followed Weed was knocked unconscious with a bottle.

The intruders carried the struggling girl off to a waiting car. Still naked from the shower, she was bundled unceremoniously into the boot, and driven away at high speed.

She had become the victim of the Symbionese Liberation Army (SLA), a shadowy terrorist organisation that had already been responsible for the murder of a schools superintendent in Oakland, California, the previous November. But this

Dragged naked from her shower

Above: The terrorists broke into the apartment Patty shared with her boyfriend. He was knocked unconscious. She was dragged naked from the apartment and hauled out to a waiting car.

Kidnap gang grab Patricia the heiress
SEE PAGE SEVEN

Left: Papers around the world rushed to report the sensational kidnap of newspaper tycoon Randolph Hearst's daughter.

was to be no ordinary kidnap. Within two months Patty Hearst, heiress to a massive fortune, would shock America by joining her captors in a violent armed bank raid. The whole nation would be arguing over whether she had done so willingly, or whether she had been the victim of brainwashing.

It wasn't long before the first ransom demand arrived at the home of Randolph Hearst. His daughter was being held in 'protective custody', and would be released only if $2 million worth of food was distributed to the poor of San Francisco. There was also a tape recording of Patty herself, telling her parents that she was all right, but that they should comply with the kidnappers' demands.

The ransom note bore the letter-head of the SLA, a seven-headed cobra, symbolising the organisation's seven aims: self-determination, co-operative production, creativity, unity, faith, purpose and collective responsibility. In other words they advocated violent revolution.

The group's leader, a black 30-year-old escaped convict named Donald DeFreeze, kept Patty in a one-room apartment on Golden Gate Avenue. She was blindfolded and bound at all times, and forced to live

Patty Hearst was a natural target for kidnap by a publicity-hungry terrorist organisation. Her grandfather had been the newspaper magnate William Randolph Hearst, immortalised in the film Citizen Kane, and anything concerning the family was headline news.

Field Marshall Cinque wasn't impressed with Hearst's efforts. He called it 'throwing a few crumbs', and demanded $4 million more. He also warned that Patty Hearst would now be kept prisoner 'until such time as the status of our captured soldiers is changed'. This was a reference to Russell Little and Joseph Remiro, SLA members who had been jailed for life for the murder of Marcus Foster.

The message from the SLA ended with another chilling warning of the danger that Patty Hearst was in. "Should any attempt be made to rescue the subject prisoner," it read, "the subject is to be executed immediately."

Despairing of police efforts to find their daughter, the Hearsts began working on their own. They were nearly arrested for accepting help from California gangster Mickey Cohen. Finally, as so many desperate relatives of kidnap victims do, they turned to mediums and psychics.

Brainwashed by gang

Then the tone of Patty's cassettes began to change. She criticised the food distribution programme as "a real disaster", and went on, "It sounds like most of the food is of low quality. No-one received any beef or lamb, and it certainly doesn't sound like the kind of food our family is used to eating."

Ten days after the food distribution began, the bombshell came. A cassette arrived from Patty, together with a photo-

and sleep in a cupboard.

DeFreeze, who styled himself 'Field Marshall Cinque' after the leader of a slave revolt in the 1830s, molested Patty sexually on one occasion, and constantly threatened to kill her. She was guarded day and night by members of the SLA, but DeFreeze's lieutenant, 23-year-old William 'Cujo' Wolfe, was kinder to the girl. Later, it was claimed that while in captivity Patty had fallen in love with him.

Free food offer

Meanwhile with $500,000 of his own money and the balance from the Foundation established by his father, William Randolph Hearst, Patty's father began the food distribution programme. Boxes of food worth around $25 a piece and containing turkey, frozen fish and chicken were handed out in the poorer districts of San Francisco. It was a shambles. During the first distribution in Oakland there were riots in the streets as people fought for the free food.

California Governor Ronald Reagan expressed his opposition to the whole programme. The future president commented that he hoped whoever ate the food would get botulism.

"Death to the Fascist insect!"

Above left: Nancy Ling Perry took part in the kidnap of Patty Hearst. She also contacted a Los Angeles radio station to announce the SLA's first attack: the murder of a schools superintendent.

Above right: Like Charles Manson, escaped convict Donald DeFreeze recruited followers from middle-class families in California. He spouted slogans copied from other terrorist groups and posed as a revolutionary fighter.

The SLA was founded by escaped convict Donald DeFreeze, and first came to public attention when its spokeswoman, Nancy Ling Perry, wrote to a local radio station claiming the organisation had been responsible for the murder of schools superintendent Marcus Foster.

DeFreeze took his inspiration for the revolutionary organisation from the gangs that ran the black prison population of California. Their watchwords were 'symbiosis' or 'team spirit'. The SLA's motto was: 'Death to the Fascist insect that preys upon the life of the people.'

Copying Argentina

In kidnapping Patty Hearst and demanding a food distribution programme, DeFreeze was imitating an Argentinian terrorist group who kidnapped Stanley Sylvester, an employee of Swift & Co., and demanded that $50,000 worth of food be handed out in the slums of Rosario in exchange for his release.

At its height the SLA had about 30 members, black and white, some drawn from good middle-class families. Later, numbers dwindled to around 12. After the culmination of the Hearst kidnap the SLA was effectively destroyed.

Harmless victim

O n 6 November 1973 Marcus A. Foster, the highly respected, black Superintendent of Schools in Oakland, California, was shot dead while walking to his car after a school board meeting. His assistant, Robert Blackburn, was also shot and badly injured.

A message was later sent to a local radio station saying that Foster and his deputy had been found guilty by a court of the people of "crimes against the children and life of the people". These 'crimes' seemed to consist primarily of steps Foster was taking to try to reduce juvenile crime. The message claimed the execution as the work of the Symbionese Liberation Army.

Cyanide crystals

Russell Little, 25, and Joseph Remiro, 28, both members of the SLA, were arrested on 10 January 1974 near Concord, California. A post-mortem revealed that Foster had been killed with bullets filled with cyanide crystals, and ballistics showed it was Remiro's gun that had fired them.

When police were called to a fire at the house of SLA spokeswoman Nancy Ling Perry, in Concord, they found guns, explosives, ammunition and cyanide, as well as SLA literature and a list of officials targeted for kidnap and murder.

Little and Remiro received life sentences for the killing of Marcus Foster.

graph showing her posing with a sub-machine gun in front of the SLA flag. "I have been issued with a 12-gauge riot shot-gun," Patty told her parents, "and I have been receiving instruction on how to use it . . . [I] will be given an issue of cyanide buckshot in order to protect myself." It was from the FBI that she was protecting herself. Patty Hearst had changed sides.

"Fighting for my freedom"

The next tape was still more explicit. On it the pretty, blonde 19-year-old sounded cool and self-possessed. "I have been given the choice," she said, "of, one, being released in a safe area, or, two, joining the forces of the Symbionese Liberation Army and fighting for my freedom and the freedom of all oppressed people. I have chosen to stay and fight."

Right: This photograph arrived at the Hearst home 10 days after the food distribution programme. Patty totes an M1 carbine in front of the SLA's flag. On a cassette sent with the photo Patty announced that she was joining the terrorists.

Just 12 days later, on Easter Monday, an armed gang held up the Hibernia Bank of California in San Francisco. They got away with $10,900, wounding two passers-by in the process. A security camera filmed the entire raid. When police took a look at the tape, they saw Donald DeFreeze and three of his followers. They also saw a young woman, wearing a black wig and holding an automatic weapon, standing in the middle of the bank. There was no doubt about it. Witnesses said she had even yelled out her name. It was Patty Hearst.

A warrant was issued for her arrest. On it she was described as 'armed and dangerous'.

On Friday 17 May 1974, following a tip-off, 150 armed police surrounded the SLA's hideout in a black district of Los Angeles. In the shoot-out that followed 6,000 shots were fired, and the police used fire bombs

Evidence

Victim or terrorist?

T he spectacle of wealthy heiress Patty Hearst robbing a bank with a gang of terrorists stunned America. To those that supported the crazed slogans of these anarchist revolutionaries, 'Tania' became an instant heroine. Others wondered if her cut-down M1 carbine was actually loaded. Was she brainwashed into joining them, forced at gunpoint — or did she take part of her own free will?

Like many SLA members, Patty Hearst adopted a new name, calling herself 'Tania'. These posters appeared at the University of California, where she had been a student.

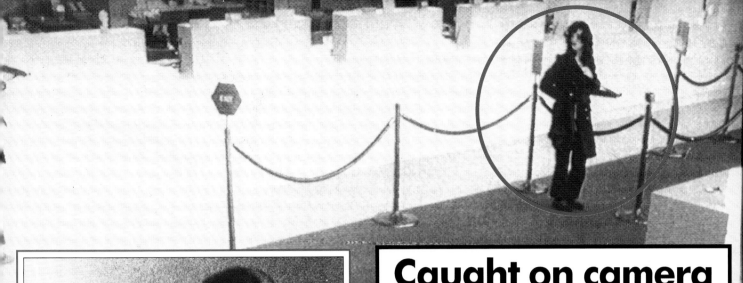

Caught on camera

A security camera recorded this image of Patty Hearst when the Symbionese Liberation Army raided the Hibernia Bank. She was under the guns of other gang members during the robbery – one can be seen on the far left of the picture. When the photograph was released, many people suspected Patty was acting under coercion. However, her subsequent career with the SLA led the FBI to regard her as one of the terrorists. The hunt for her was intensified and she was eventually arrested in 1975.

Left: Another clip from the security camera system shows Patty with one hand in her pocket and carbine over her shoulder during the robbery. It remains a mystery why she was wearing a dark wig. Was she trying to disguise herself? If so, why stand directly in front of the cameras?

The FBI released this picture of Patty Hearst in 1975. According to FBI reports she had changed her appearance while on the run, cutting her hair short and dyeing it.

developed for warfare in Vietnam. The building was burned to the ground.

Inside were found the bodies of DeFreeze and Wolfe, as well as those of four women members of the SLA: Nancy Ling Perry, Patricia 'Mizmoon' Soltysik, Camilla 'Gabi' Hall and Angela 'Gelina' Atwood. All were in their twenties.

Patty arrested

But Patty Hearst had not been there. It wasn't until 16 months later that she was arrested in San Francisco with two other members of the now-defunct SLA, William and Emily Harris. The first pictures of Patty showed her giving the clenched fist salute of defiance. Like other SLA members she now had a *nom-de-guerre*. She was calling herself 'Tania'.

It had been her parents' contention throughout the long months that Patty had been brainwashed into joining the SLA. "I think that after 60 days you can change people," her father told reporters. But the prosecution at Patty Hearst's trial argued that she had been a willing participant in the bank robbery.

A battle of the experts ensued. Dr Donald Lunde, author of a study on mass murderers, and Dr Seymour Pollack, prosecution witness at the trial of Sirhan Sirhan for the murder of Bobby Kennedy, appeared for the state. The Hearsts recruited Dr Louis Jolyon West, an expert on brainwashing, to speak in Patty's defence.

West told the court: "If a person who has been subject to extreme or unusual stress commits an illegal act in the belief that it is necessary for the preservation of their life,

that mental state must be taken into account by the court."

Patty's description of her captivity – the 60 days blindfolded in a cupboard, the abuse and the threats – was confirmed in its entirety by a lie-detector test. The controversy raged worldwide. Writing in the London *Times*, one psychologist claimed that studies of wartime prisoners had shown a mere 30 days of such treatment could produce breakdown and 'inhibitory reverse', in which the subject's behaviour and ideas become the reverse of normal.

On the other hand there were some who suggested Patty Hearst had helped to stage her own kidnapping, and the security tape showing her wielding a weapon in the lobby of the bank was a powerful witness for the prosecution.

Guilty of bank robbery

Although it was argued in court that the tape seemed to show DeFreeze and the others covering Patty with their weapons, and although she claimed she had been told to stand directly under the camera and shout out her name, the jury were unconvinced. They found Patty Hearst guilty of bank robbery and use of a firearm in commission of a felony. She was sentenced to seven years in jail.

But that wasn't the end of the story. On 19 November 1976 she was released on

Above: Patty Hearst gives a clenched fist salute after her arrest with two other members of the SLA in September 1975.

Left: Patty Hearst arrives at court, charged with bank robbery and use of a firearm in commission of a felony. Her lawyers argued that she had been forced into joining the gang.

The Trial

Attacked by gang leader

There were several bizarre terrorist groups active in the USA at the time — all spouting fashionable revolutionary slogans. Often led by convicted criminals, most of these groups managed to attract recruits from impressionable young people in California. Was Patty just another teenager under their spell? In court she told a different story, alleging that gang leader Donald DeFreeze had sexually assaulted her. He had been killed two years previously with other members of the SLA when their hideout was burned to the ground by police.

Freed to marry her bodyguard

After having her sentence cut on appeal, Patty was pardoned by President Carter. She later married her bodyguard Bernard Shaw, seen here together with their daughter Gillian. She has always maintained that her role in the bank robbery was staged. She had been forced to stand directly in line with the security cameras and even to shout out her name in case the pictures were not clear enough.

$1.5 million bail pending appeal, and the superior court judge ultimately reduced her sentence to five years' probation, commenting that there could not be "a heart in America that was not full of compassion" for her parents. To complete her rehabilitation, Patty Hearst received a presidential pardon from Jimmy Carter.

In what some have seen as a parallel to the way she had come so disastrously under the spell of the SLA, Patty Hearst later married her bodyguard. □

Sympathy for the Devil

Psychologists argued that Patty Hearst was suffering from Stockholm Syndrome when she took part in the raid on the Hibernia Bank. This strange affection that some victims develop for their kidnappers was named after a case in Stockholm in 1973.

Jan-Erik Olsson took two girls hostage during a failed bank raid, and held them for six days. The girls soon began to identify more with their captor than with those trying to rescue them. One let Olsson caress her breasts and hips, and long afterwards both said they still felt close to their former captor. Olsson also said he couldn't have killed his hostages, because he felt too close to them.

Dependent on captors

The psychological explanation for this phenomenon is that the victim returns to a childlike state of dependency on the captor. Unable to bear the stress of being a victim, he or she then prefers to identify with the captor, seeing him not so much as a criminal, but as someone who needs understanding. Female hostages may sometimes have sex with their captors in order to gain their protection.

For the kidnapper, it becomes psychologically harder to murder a victim he has come to know personally. Statistics suggest that a kidnap victim who survives the first three days has a much better chance of coming out alive.

Staying aloof from victims

Having become aware of the syndrome, professional kidnappers began to take pains to avoid intimacy with their victims. While anyone thought in danger of being kidnapped is now advised to try to strike up a relationship as quickly as possible with their captors, perhaps by telling stories about their childhood or family.

Above: Kristin Ehnvap, 21, was one of the women taken hostage during a failed bank raid in Stockholm. The captives' behaviour under stress became known as the 'Stockholm Syndrome'.

Below: Jan-Erik Olsson is taken away by police after his surrender.

'AIR RAID'
VICTIM WAS STRANGLED

In 1942 a skeleton was found in a ruined church. But it did not look like another victim of the German bombers: this was a murder.

It was 17 July 1942, during the height of the World War II blitz on London, and demolition workers were clearing rubble from the site of a Baptist church at 302 Kennington Road, south-east London, near the Oval cricket ground. The church had been bombed in August 1940. Now the crew's pick-axes were prising up one of the stone slabs in what had been a cellar floor under the church vestry.

Beneath the slab was a human skeleton. As the workers lifted it up, the head appeared to break off. Another victim of the German air raids, they thought, and reported their grisly find to the police.

Divisional Detective Inspector Frederick Hatton and his deputy, Detective Inspector John Keeling, however, thought differently. First, there wasn't a crater; second, it seemed very improbable that a bomb blast could have lifted a weighty stone slab, put the victim in a shallow grave under it, then neatly replaced the slab. Human agency must have been involved. So the policemen made a parcel of the

bones, some with parchment-like flesh still clinging to them, took it to Southwark Mortuary, and informed the local coroner.

The next day the Home Office pathologist, Professor Keith Simpson, examined the skeleton, which was complete except for pieces of the limbs. That the victim was female was evident from the dried-up womb in the lower trunk. The pathologist also ruled out the possibility of death by bomb blast: the skull had not been broken off by the demolition crew, it had been *cut* off. Also, both arms had been cut off at the

The murderer left his victim in a bombed-out building at a time when over 200 German bombers (above) were attacking Britain every night. London was full of bomb sites ideal for disposing of a body.

Over 40,000 people died in the German bombing attacks on Britain. The raids demolished 100,000 buildings, which would not be rebuilt while the war continued. Whoever murdered the woman found in Kennington Road had obviously hoped it would not be discovered for many years.

Left inset: Sticks laid on the ground in the corner of the church cellar mark the unknown woman's secret grave.

the limbs, but without success. What the team did find, however, was more of the yellowish deposit found on the skeleton. The Home Office analyst, Mr J. Ryffel, revealed it to be slaked quicklime.

In using this, the murderer had made a fundamental error. For although quicklime is caustic, when it is mixed with water to form slaked quicklime it has no 'burning' effect. And by killing maggots and beetles, the slaked quicklime had actually helped to preserve the body – quite the opposite to what the murderer had intended!

Throat preserved

It was in this way that the injuries to the victim's throat and larynx had been preserved. Professor Simpson was able to dissect the larynx and examine it under a microscope. The upper horn of the thyroid cartilage on the right side had been fractured and part of the bone pressed inwards towards the windpipe, causing bruising. Around the fracture was a small dried-up blood clot. The bruising and blood clot could have occurred only while the person was alive – and the nature of the injuries pointed to death by strangulation.

ferred to his laboratory at Guy's Hospital. He could have had no idea then that he was embarking on what was to become a classic case of forensic detection.

With the police, he spent the next two days sifting through the earth under the church cellar floor for the missing pieces of

No arms, no legs

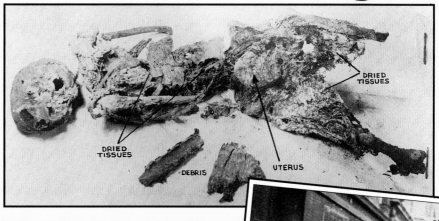

DRIED TISSUES

DRIED TISSUES

DEBRIS

UTERUS

Professor Keith Simpson (right, centre) immediately recognised that the mystery woman's body had been dismembered. The head had been cut off, not broken off by the workman when the corpse was uncovered. The arms and legs had also been neatly severed.

Identification problems

Bomb blasts can produce very strange injuries, but there was no doubt that someone had deliberately removed parts of the body to make identification difficult. The left humerus was present, which helped Simpson calculate that the murder victim was at least five feet and half an inch tall. The skull belonged to a 40- to 50-year-old woman. Most significantly, Simpson found the voice box preserved and the thyroid cartilage was damaged in a way that can only occur during strangulation.

elbows, and both legs cut off at the knees. No bomb could have been that selective in its destruction. The victim had been dismembered.

Hands and feet removed

Professor Simpson estimated that the woman had been dead for 12 to 18 months, which meant that death had occurred some six months *after* the church had been bombed. Her killer had also tried to destroy means of identification by removing the face, eyes, hands and feet, scalp and hair; but Professor Simpson found one strand of hair – dark brown with grey – stuck to the back of the skull. There was also a yellowish deposit on the skull and neck area, and signs of blackening by fire on the skull, hip and knees.

The question was: could the body be identified from what little remained? Professor Simpson said he would do his utmost and had the mummified remains trans-

Hatton and Keeling were accustomed to cases of strangulation being identified by the classic signs of finger imprint and suffocation – so could Professor Simpson be certain?

"Yes," he told them. "This little bone never gets broken, alone, except when the neck is gripped tight by a strangling hand. It is the pressure of the fingertip or thumb that does it." And he added that he had found another possible bruise on the back of the head, which he thought could have been caused by the head striking the ground when the throat was gripped, or by a fall.

X-ray evidence

How old had the woman been? From X-ray photographs of her skull the pathologist was able to check the amount of closure of the skull sutures, or plates, which fuse together at regular periods from the teenage years to old age. He found that the brow sutures had joined together, fusion was still happening between the top sutures, and there was no fusion yet between the two groups of sutures – which meant she was aged between 40 and 50.

Next, he had to establish her height. Because her skeleton was incomplete, this was not so straightforward. Simpson used two methods. The first was to re-assemble the skeleton and make appropriate allowances for the missing bone and the soft tissue in the knee joints and the soles and heels of the feet. From that he estimated height at between 5 ft ¼ in and 5 ft ¾ in.

The second method was to use Pearson's formulae and Rollet's tables, both of which give estimates of height based on one of the long bones of the limbs – in this case, the dead woman's left humerus. The Pearson's estimate came out at 5 ft ½ in to 5 ft 1 in. Rollet's tables, considered a less reliable guide, said 4 ft 10 in to 4 ft 10½ in. Simpson took 5 ft ½ in as the woman's probable height.

More clues were emerging. In the uterus Professor Simpson found a benign fibroid tumour, three to four inches in diameter. The upper jaw was equally revealing – four teeth, molars, three of them with fillings; claw marks of a dental plate; and signs of bone-thickening around the back teeth. All of this could be checked against her medical and dental records, if they could be traced.

The police now had something positive to go on: a woman between 40 and 50, about 5 ft ½ in tall, with dark-brown hair going grey, who would have been reported missing 12 to 18 months previously.

After hours of checking through police records of missing persons they came up with a name that fitted – Mrs Rachel Dobkin. Her sister, Polly Dubinsky, had reported her disappearance to police on 12 April 1941.

Suspicious fire

Rachel was the wife of Harry Dobkin, 49, who at that time had been a firewatcher at 302 Kennington Lane. Was this merely coincidence, or something more sinister?

Detective Inspector Keeling's visit to Polly Dubinsky paid off immediately. Polly told him that her sister Rachel was 47, had dark hair going grey, and had been to the London Hospital for treatment for "something in her womb". The clincher was Rachel's height: "Five foot one inch, the same as me," Polly said. And she had a full-face photograph of Rachel.

Polly had last seen her sister on 11 April 1941, Good Friday. Rachel had said she was going to see her estranged husband, Harry, about his maintenance arrears. (A maintenance order had been made against him in 1923 of £1 a week.)

Arranged marriage

Rachel had married Dobkin at Bethnal Green Synagogue in 1920. It was an arranged marriage, in accordance with Jewish tradition, but the union lasted less than a week. The maintenance order fared no better; between 1923 and 1941 Dobkin was frequently in arrears, and non-payment once landed him a short prison sentence. Several times Rachel took out summonses against him for assault during confrontations over the arrears.

Later that day, the 11th, Rachel had met Dobkin for tea in a cafe in Dalston; a

Evidence

"Those are

From 1934 to 1940 Rachel Dobkin had received dental treatment from Mr Barnett Kopkin of north London. He kept meticulous records and was able to draw a diagram of Rachel's upper jaw as it had been when he had last treated her, including the fillings he had made.

Dental diagram

When police compared this diagram with the skull in Professor Simpson's laboratory the result was conclusive – the teeth and fillings were in the correct positions, there was the same gap for the denture, and the same claw marks. And when Mr Kopkin saw the skull for himself he immediately confirmed that the dental work was his own. Also, he said that when he had extracted two of Rachel's teeth on the left side of the upper jaw he might well have left some small root ends (not unusual in extractions).

Root fragments

Guy's leading dental surgeon, Sir William Kelsey Fry, had X-ray films made of the upper jaw – and there were the residual root fragments, just as the dentist had predicted.

waitress saw them leave together at 6.30 p.m. Rachel was never seen alive again.

The next day, 12 April, Rachel's handbag, which contained her identity card and ration book, was found in a post office in

Skull had been smashed

Harry Dobkin was hired as a fire-watcher by a firm of solicitors next door to the burned-out Baptist church. It was his job to keep an eye on the premises overnight. Firemen were summoned to a small blaze in the ruined church one night in April 1941 by a patrolling policeman. When they arrived, Dobkin blurted out that he hadn't started the fire.

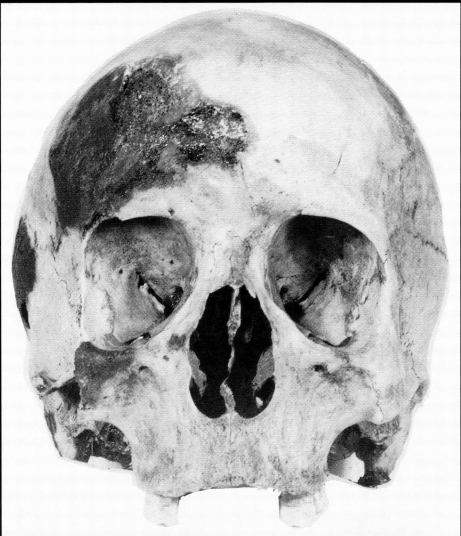

The scalp and hair had been removed before the body was buried. The face and lower jaw had been smashed, but the rest of the skull was intact. There were enough teeth in the upper jaw for the woman's identity to be proved if her dental records could be found. Simpson also decided to try the photographic identification method that was used in the Ruxton case in 1935.

my fillings!"

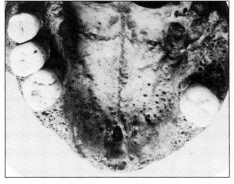

The lower jaw was missing, but the upper jaw retained several molars, three of them filled. There were also marks from the claws of a dental plate. Once the woman was tentatively identified as Rachel Dobkin, her dentist was located. Barnett Kopkin recognised his own work immediately.

Guildford, Surrey. That afternoon Polly learned that Rachel had not been home. She reported her missing to the London police, telling them she thought Harry Dobkin was responsible for her disappearance. However, Britain was at war and London's authorities were at full stretch coping with the disruption of the almost nightly bombing raids. Consequently, Dobkin wasn't interviewed until 16 April. In the meantime, on the night of 14/15 April, a mysterious fire broke out in the cellar of the ruined Baptist church. The fire – a blazing mattress – was soon put out by the fire brigade. Strangely, the fire-watcher, Harry Dobkin, did not raise the alarm; that was done by a patrolling constable. But Dobkin was there when the firemen arrived and, without being asked, he blurted out that he hadn't started the blaze.

On 16 April Dobkin told police he worked as a fire-watcher for a firm of solicitors, keeping watch on a building adjoining 302 Kennington Lane, where they stored legal

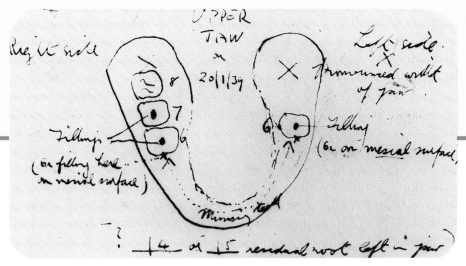

67

papers and documents. He patrolled the firm's store room at regular intervals through the night; in between patrols he relaxed in a chair in a bombed house next door. He made a statement that after he and Rachel had left the Dalston cafe, he had taken her to catch her bus home, and he hadn't seen her since.

The police were not satisfied, and suspected that Dobkin had started the fire in the church. They searched the premises and dug up part of the floor, uncovering a freshly dug trench, six feet by two feet. It was empty.

Medical records

Rachel's photograph was circulated in newspapers and the *Police Gazette*, but no-one came forward with information as to her whereabouts.

But now, in August 1942, 16 months after her disappearance, police were close to solving the mystery. They talked to Rachel's doctor, Dr M. Watson, who had diagnosed the uterine fibroid growth at Mildmay Mission Hospital, Bethnal Green, in 1939. Dr Watson had sent Rachel to the London Hospital for treatment. Records there showed that she had refused to have the growth operated on. Rachel's dentist, Mr Barnett Kopkin, of north London, was able to produce her complete dental records. And the photograph of Rachel when superimposed on a photograph of her skull was a perfect match. The net was

finally beginning to tighten around Harry Dobkin.

Dobkin was now living in Dalston; his fire-watching job had ended in May 1942, when the solicitors had moved their store room elsewhere.

News of the skeleton find had not yet been released to the newspapers, but Dobkin must have known something was going on; for on 4 August – three weeks after the skeleton had been dug up – he was seen on the premises by a constable at 6 a.m. Had Dobkin been looking for Rachel's grave?

On 26 August Detective Inspector Hatton made his move. He asked Dobkin to assist in his enquiries. He took him to the cellar, pointed to the spot where the demolition crew had unearthed his wife's body and told him she had been strangled.

"I wouldn't strangle a woman," Dobkin told him. "I wouldn't hit a woman. Some men might, but I wouldn't." And although he had spent over a year on the site as a fire-watcher, Dobkin swore he hadn't known of the cellar's existence. He also denied having been back to the bombed church after his job ended in May. Hatton then called in the constable, who immediately identified Dobkin as the man he had seen on the premises on 4 August. "I know him well," the constable added. "I've spoken to him several times."

Dobkin cried: "He's lying! He's lying! I've never seen him before. And I wasn't there."

Forensics

How the face

To establish the identity of the skull Professor Simpson, with the help of Guy's Photographic Department, used a technique pioneered by Professor Glaister and Professor Brash in the celebrated case of Dr Buck Ruxton: in 1935 Ruxton was hanged for killing his wife and her maid and dismembering their bodies.

Skull photographed

First, Rachel Dobkin's skull was photographed. Next, the full-face portrait of Rachel that her sister had supplied was photographed and then enlarged to the same size as the skull. The two images were then superimposed: they corresponded exactly. At Dobkin's trial Professor Simpson said of the superimposition: "The general contour of the skull was the same, allowing for scalp thickness; the contour of the cheeks, allowing for flesh, was the same. The position and shape of the upper jaw was the same; the position, height and width of the nose space were the same and fitted perfectly."

Undoubtedly, the skull was that of Rachel Dobkin.

Hatton charged Dobkin with his wife's murder.

Dobkin's trial opened at the Old Bailey on 17 November 1942. Dobkin's counsel,

Harry and Rachel Dobkin were married at Bethnal Green Synagogue in 1920. But the marriage had been arranged by their families and was doomed to last less than a week after the ceremony. For the next 20 years Rachel Dobkin pursued Harry for maintenance payments, often in court.

fitted

Simpson obtained several photographs of Rachel Dobkin and compared her face to the shape of the skull.

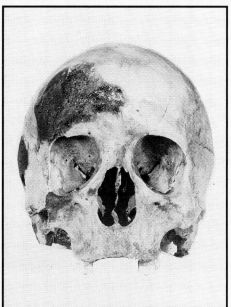

Although Dobkin had burned part of the head and had removed most of the teeth, the basic shape of the skull was intact when workmen recovered it from the cellar.

When a negative image of the skull was superimposed onto a photo of Rachel Dobkin, it matched exactly. Simpson described it as fitting "like a mask".

Mr F. H. Lawton, fought every medico-legal point of the prosecution's case, despite advice not to challenge Professor Simpson's formidable identification evidence. (The prosecution submitted scores of photographs and notes, every photograph taken and prepared by Miss Mary Newman, head of Guy's Photographic Department, to support the pathologist's findings.)

Desperate defence

One line of Lawton's attack was to suggest to Professor Simpson that Rachel Dobkin might have been thrown to the ground by a bomb blast, and that in falling could have hit her voice-box on masonry or something similar. "Is it not possible – I do not put it any higher than that – that a fall under those circumstances might break the horn of the right thyroid?" asked Lawton.

Professor Simpson replied that he had seen such injuries many times, but none had ever been confined to a fracture of the horn, as in Rachel Dobkin's case, adding that in 15 years he had examined more than 11,000 cases "and I have never seen this injury except in manual strangulation."

Was he saying it was impossible? Lawton asked. To which Simpson replied: "I say that I have never seen it; and I have seen many falls and many strangulations."

Professor Simpson's expert testimony was too detailed and accumulative to be argued away. The jury returned a verdict of guilty after only 20 minutes. Dobkin was hanged at Wandsworth Prison on 27 January 1943. □

Hanged for murder

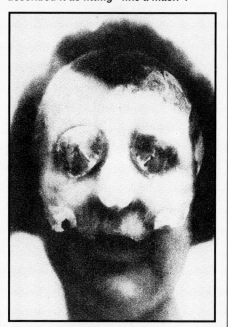

Harry Dobkin's attempts to conceal the murder of his wife failed miserably. By watering down the quicklime, he actually helped preserve the body. No-one was going to believe the woman had been killed in an air raid, because he had chopped her hands and feet off and left the corpse underneath a stone slab in the cellar.

The case against Harry Dobkin was damning. His defence was reduced to suggesting that the telltale signs of strangulation might have occurred during a bomb blast.

Then Dobkin entered the witness box himself, and went to pieces under cross-examination. He alternated between bluster and panic and ended up accusing all the prosecution witnesses of lying. One observer wrote: "I have seldom seen quite so grim a portrayal of a man betraying absolute guilt by a sort of gradual disintegration in which the shrivelled little soul was finally stripped bare of all pretence."

LEFT TO LINGERING DEATH BY KILLER DOCTOR

She was saved by a miracle. Her throat had been cut in such a way that she would take hours to die. But Madhu Baksh lived to testify against her evil husband.

Dr Madhu Baksh was the victim of a cold-blooded murder plot. Pumped full of morphine, she was left helpless and bleeding to death in woods near her home.

The surgeons worked frantically on the dying woman on the operating table in front of them. A gaping knife wound in her throat nearly five inches across had exposed her windpipe, slashing through a main artery, neck muscles and nerves.

It was a massive injury. By rights the woman, herself a doctor, should have been long dead. She had lost a lot of blood, four to five pints. But Dr Madhu Baksh was

going to survive. Her life had been saved by a minor miracle, some would say two.

Dr Baksh, drugged and with her throat cut, had been dumped in a Kent woodland to die. But her would-be killer had made one minor miscalculation. Saturday 4 January 1985 was one of the coldest nights of that winter, and as Dr Baksh's life ebbed away in the undergrowth by Keston Ponds, near Bromley, the temperature dropped below freezing. Hypothermia set

in, her pulse slowed, and the blood that had been pumping out of the wound slowed to a trickle. Severed ends of blood vessels began to coagulate, stemming her blood loss still further.

Frogs and toads

Now minor miracle number two was about to happen. In the pitch dark on a sub-zero night there was actually someone else

70

Biography

Love in the surgery

Dr John Baksh was a wealthy GP who had insured the life of his second wife, Madhu, for £315,000. They had met at his Kent practice (above), and his first wife mysteriously died shortly after he and Madhu became lovers.

Madhu Baksh met her husband in 1980, when she joined his profitable surgery in Chislehurst. He was married with two children, and she was recently divorced and also had two children. Within weeks of Madhu's arrival, he began to court her. Their relationship deepened, and he was soon promising to leave his wife for her. Then, in December 1982, he went on holiday with his wife to Spain, where she suffered a fatal heart attack. Dr Baksh wasted no time in proposing marriage to Madhu; giving her his first wife's wedding ring two weeks later.

and Chislehurst. He told detectives his wife had been abducted near their home while driving his car. His BMW, with the personalised plates JB 70, had been found abandoned in Bromley. Baksh wrung his hands and asked detectives: "Who could do such a thing to my poor wife?"

Dark secrets

Barely conscious, Madhu fixed her husband with her gaze. They both knew dark secrets they could not speak of. Madhu because her wounds meant she could not; John because he dare not.

Madhu was determined to survive. She wanted to tell police that it was her own husband who had drugged her, cut her throat, driven her to the woods and left her to die. And she wanted to tell them what had happened to his first wife.

As Madhu improved, her husband came to see her several times a day, bringing flowers and magazines. John Baksh was desperate. While his wife could not speak he was safe. When she was able to, it was

in the wood. Ecologist Dr Keith Corbett had a passionate interest in frogs and toads. The ponds in the woodland were home to large numbers of both species. The icy moonlit night was ideal for seeing them in their natural habitat.

Dr Corbett heard a faint moan coming from the tangled undergrowth. In the beam of his torch he saw a woman's legs sticking out from under a bush.

In the intensive care unit at Bromley Hospital detectives waited to interview 43-year-old Dr Baksh. Getting any information would be difficult. Her vocal cords had been damaged and it would be several weeks before she could say much at all. She was too weak to write down replies to their questions.

A life-support machine was needed to keep her going. Now and then, with a supreme effort, she managed to croak out the odd word. Medical staff thought she had said the names of the synthetic heroin substitutes Methadone and Omnopon. One was sure he had heard her say "Morphine". It was mentioned to the police. Perhaps she was trying to convey that her abductors had been after drugs. Doctors had been attacked before in south London for their supplies. They would have to be patient and wait for all the details.

Her husband came to her bedside. Dr John Baksh was also a well-known local GP. The couple ran two large practices together in the London suburbs of Bickley

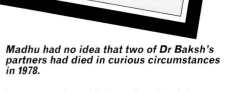

Madhu had no idea that two of Dr Baksh's partners had died in curious circumstances in 1978.

important she told the police the right story to get him off the hook.

As a policewoman sat in the same room guarding Madhu, John embraced her and kissed her. He asked his wife: "Do you remember the masked men who dragged you out of your car?" Madhu glared back. She pointed to him, indicating that she knew it was he who had knifed her. He whispered to her that the police were coming to take her statement later that day and that their stories had to be the same or the detec-

Evil Mind

In May 1983 Dr Baksh took Madhu to Paris for a romantic weekend. He confessed that the death of his first wife (below) had not been an accident. "I sacrificed Ruby for you," he told her.

Confession in Paris

Five months after proposing to her, Dr Baksh took Madhu to Paris. In their hotel bedroom he made the astonishing confession that he had murdered his first wife. Stunned by her fiancé's admission, Madhu realised that there was no-one she could tell. Dr Baksh was a respected GP; who would have believed such an incredible story? She decided to remain silent, and in due course married Dr Baksh. Little did she realise that she would become his next victim.

tives would soon smell a rat. He begged her: "Save me, save my life, or I will go to jail." As he got up to leave he told her: "Two masked men – remember?"

As soon as he left the room Madhu reached for a chalk board used for scribbling messages to the nurses. She wrote: "My husband is a killer; tell the judges he killed his first wife." She handed the board to the policewoman.

Later on, Detective Superintendent Norman Stockford read Madhu's statement with growing amazement. Her story was more like something from the pages of an Agatha Christie novel than the files of the Metropolitan Police.

Charming and attractive

She told how she and her husband had met when she joined his practice in 1980. Madhu was a divorcée. She had two children from an arranged marriage that had gone wrong. Right from the start Baksh made advances to her. She found him undeniably charming and attractive, but resisted because he was married with two children of his own.

Gradually she fell under his spell. Baksh told her he planned to divorce Ruby, but shortly after that his wife died from an apparent heart attack. Baksh proposed to Madhu just a fortnight later, on New Year's Day 1983, while they were on holiday in

Spain. Madhu accepted the marriage offer. Baksh gave her Ruby's wedding ring, kissed her and told her: "You are mine now."

In May 1983 the lovers went for a romantic weekend to Paris. After a night on the town they returned to their room at the luxurious Montparnasse Parc hotel and went to bed. Suddenly Baksh confessed that his wife had not died of a heart attack. He told Madhu: "I sacrificed Ruby for you. I killed her."

He then told his fiancée how he had drugged his wife by spiking her bedtime drink with sleeping tablets. When Ruby had fallen into a deep sleep he killed her with a massive injection of heroin into her thigh. He had then conned an elderly Spanish doctor into believing she had died of a heart attack. The couple were only three days from their 21st wedding anniversary.

Madhu had been terrified but, despite the amazing confession, she had gone ahead with the wedding. She told detectives: "I was too scared not to."

Detective Superintendent Stockford had to take two courses of action immediately. Blood taken from Madhu before transfusions saved her life had to be checked to see if Baksh had drugged her. And the Foreign Office and Interpol had to be contacted. Stockford wanted urgent permission from the Spanish authorities to exhume the corpse of Ruby Baksh, which had been buried in a hillside tomb near Mojacar.

He was going to charge Baksh with attempting to murder Madhu. If the tests on Ruby showed signs of morphine he would also charge him with her murder.

At the police laboratories in Lambeth Dr John Taylor, a Scotland Yard toxicologist, tested a tiny sample of blood taken from Madhu when she was admitted to Bromley Hospital casualty department. It showed a massive quantity of morphine.

Body exhumed

On 8 June Stockford arrived in Spain with Home Office pathologist Dr Iain West. Supervised by a local investigating magistrate, gravediggers took two and a half hours to free the coffin from its resting place. When the coffin was opened the body of Ruby Baksh was found to have been well preserved. It had been wrapped in plastic sheeting, which had helped to mummify the remains. Dr West was able to take a portion of tissue from the liver and other organs. They were flown back to the Scotland Yard labs, where tests proved conclusively that she had been given a huge overdose of morphine.

Baksh, already remanded in custody over the attack on Madhu, was charged with the murder of Ruby at Bow Street Magistrates on 28 August 1986. The case against him was becoming stronger and stronger. When Madhu was released from hospital she went home and found a used syringe and the wrappers from five ampoules of morphine. Clearly her hus-

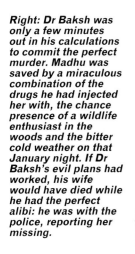

Right: Dr Baksh was only a few minutes out in his calculations to commit the perfect murder. Madhu was saved by a miraculous combination of the drugs he had injected her with, the chance presence of a wildlife enthusiast in the woods and the bitter cold weather on that January night. If Dr Baksh's evil plans had worked, his wife would have died while he had the perfect alibi: he was with the police, reporting her missing.

Below: After Madhu's revelations to the police, the authorities decided to exhume the body of Ruby Baksh, which was buried in Mojacar in Spain. The corpse of the doctor's unfortunate first wife was well-preserved, due, in part, to the plastic sheeting it was wrapped in. Forensic tests revealed that Ruby had received a massive overdose of morphine.

Standard special on the terrible secrets of the

THE LONDON EVENING STAND...

Minutes from a perfect murder

by Patrick McGowan

WHEN HE attacked his wife, Madhu, Dr John Baksh came within 30 minutes of committing the second perfect murder, according to the detective leading the case.

Madhu escaped death by a hairsbreadth from the horrific throat wounds inflicted by her husband.

She survived her injuries thanks to a unique combination of circumstances.

In cutting her throat, Dr Baksh slashed through her vocal cords and windpipe, but did not sever the major arteries of the neck.

He did this quite deliberately so she would survive a number of hours after he reported her missing.

Meanwhile he would have an excellent alibi, as the police would be at his house along with relatives at the time he intended she would die.

Gasping

All that evening as he played the distraught husband to detectives, Madhu Baksh's life was slowly slipping away as she lay behind a bush near Keston Ponds.

She had been bleeding to death for over seven hours and would have been lucky to survive another 30 minutes when she was saved by the arrival at the remote beauty spot of a naturalist looking for toads.

Keston Ponds are quiet enough in daytime during the winter months.

At 1 a.m. on a bitter January morning they are deserted except for this one occasion.

The naturalist heard a gasping, gurgling sound and went to investigate believing he might find an injured animal.

Instead he found Madhu Baksh and her life was saved —just.

By all normal medical reckoning she should have died several hours earlier, but three factors combined to keep her alive.

The bitter cold that night—it was the coldest night so far that year—had slowed down the rate at which she lost blood. The low temperatures helped to thicken and coagulate the blood streaming from her neck wound.

Secondly the severity of the injury to her windpipe helped to keep her alive. Patients with throat injuries can choke to death.

In her case the wound acted as a crude tracheotomy—she was able to suck in vital oxygen through the hole in her neck.

The third factor in her survival is possibly the most ironic for the doctor husband who tried to kill her.

In order to subdue her while he drove to Keston Ponds and then attacked her, Dr Baksh injected her with a large dose of morphine.

While this stopped her from resisting his attack it also had the effect of preventing the onset of clinical shock which would have killed her.

As it was, she came as close as it is possible to come to dying both at Keston Ponds and in the hours following her admission to Bromley Hospital.

Shock

Det Supt Norman Stockford, who led the investigation, said: "It was almost a miracle that Madhu was found at that time in the morning.

"Had her body been found the following day the pathologist would have been able to give only an approximate time of death and Mr Baksh would have claimed he was already being interviewed by police at the time she died.

"It is quite clear from the way he cut her throat that he intended she would die slowly for just this reason."

...E ... Dr Madhu Baksh: "I had ...ve for my husband."

Ruby was murdered

Dr Baksh told Madhu how he murdered his first wife. He said he had put sleeping tablets in Ruby's drink, rendering her unconscious. Then he injected a massive quantity of heroin into her thigh, killing her that night. He persuaded an elderly Spanish doctor that she had suffered a heart attack, and, without any serious investigation, Ruby was buried in Spain.

Above: Ruby Baksh died while she and her husband were on holiday in Spain, three days before their 21st wedding anniversary. John Baksh had administered a drug overdose while she was asleep.

soon found the answer. Baksh was investing over £1,000 a week on insurance policies on his wife's life. Despite their £90,000 a year joint income, Baksh was heavily in debt. He had an income tax demand for £7,000, a pressing overdraft of £2,000, and he owed school fees totalling around £2,000.

The insurance policies were massive. As things stood, had his plot to do away with Madhu been successful, he would have received a £315,000 pay out. Stockford was hardly surprised to learn that Dr Baksh had received nearly £100,000 in insurance payouts when his first wife died.

Old Bailey trial

The trial of Dr Baksh opened at the Old Bailey on 9 December 1986. Baksh pleaded not guilty. His defence: that Ruby's death had been suicide, and that Madhu's cut throat had been an accident.

Madhu gave evidence against the man she had once loved. She told the jury of the night in Paris he had confessed to murder. She said: "After he finished telling me about how he had murdered his wife, he calmly rolled over, went to sleep, and actually started snoring.

"I was left with a mixture of fury, disbelief and depression. A few weeks later I

band had not been expecting her back. The items were added to the growing file of evidence.

The detectives had pieced together the how of the case, but what of the why? What had been Baksh's motive for wanting his new wife out of the way? Murder squad officers looking into the couple's finances

asked him why he had done it. He said: 'If I had not done it I would not have you.' I was frightened for my life. I realised if he had done it to her, he could do it to me, too. I wanted to tell someone but he was a highly respected man; no-one would have believed me."

When Madhu told Baksh of her fears for her own safety, he wept and told her: "How can you be so cruel? What I have done is the biggest sacrifice anyone can do for love."

Morphine injection

The jury also heard how, on the day he tried to take her life, Baksh had taken Madhu to buy diamond jewellery to celebrate their forthcoming wedding anniversary. When they got home he opened a bottle of champagne. While Madhu's back was turned he slipped a sleeping draught into the fizzing wine. With Madhu in a stupor he injected her with a huge dose of morphine, then drove her to the woodland at Keston Ponds and slit her throat with a kitchen knife.

In his defence Baksh told the court that he had made up the story about killing his first wife to demonstrate how much he loved Madhu. Of the attack on Madhu he said that they had had a row and Madhu had threatened him with the kitchen knife. He said: "I took the knife from her and she calmed down. Later she had a pain in her chest and I gave her a morphine jab.

"Later we decided to drive to see some friends to get advice about our problems. I put the knife in my pocket to show it to them. We got out of the car for some fresh air at Keston Ponds. Madhu asked me where the knife was. I pointed it at her throat because I wanted her to know what it felt like to be threatened with a knife. She pushed at it with her left hand; it was the pressure of her hand that pushed the knife into her neck."

Baksh said he had not called for help because he was confused. But he freely told the astonished jury that after going home he thought he had left a glove at the scene, and he drove back to Keston Ponds where he checked up on his wife as she lay bleeding to death. He told the court: "She seemed to be breathing all right."

The jury was not taken in by his preposterous defence. He was convicted on both charges. The judge, Recorder of London Sir James Miskin, sentenced him to life for the murder of Ruby and to 14 years for the attack on Madhu, recommending he serve a minimum of 20 years. He told him: "You killed Ruby skilfully to gratify your lust for Madhu. You are a danger to those close to you and the public at large." □

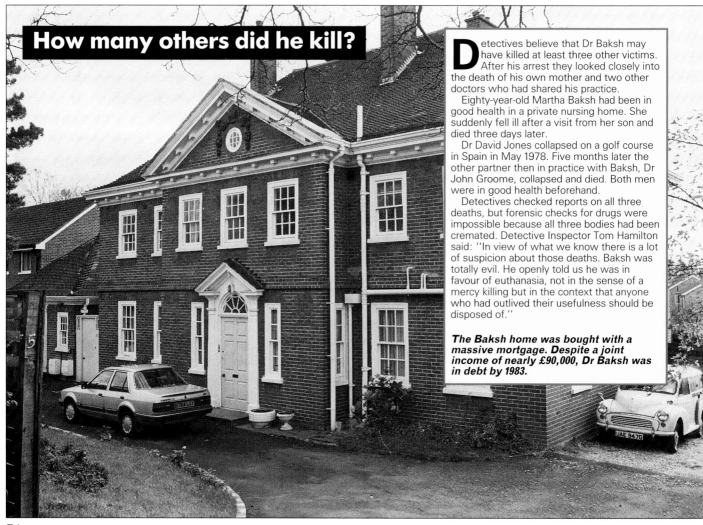

How many others did he kill?

Detectives believe that Dr Baksh may have killed at least three other victims. After his arrest they looked closely into the death of his own mother and two other doctors who had shared his practice.

Eighty-year-old Martha Baksh had been in good health in a private nursing home. She suddenly fell ill after a visit from her son and died three days later.

Dr David Jones collapsed on a golf course in Spain in May 1978. Five months later the other partner then in practice with Baksh, Dr John Groome, collapsed and died. Both men were in good health beforehand.

Detectives checked reports on all three deaths, but forensic checks for drugs were impossible because all three bodies had been cremated. Detective Inspector Tom Hamilton said: "In view of what we know there is a lot of suspicion about those deaths. Baksh was totally evil. He openly told us he was in favour of euthanasia, not in the sense of a mercy killing but in the context that anyone who had outlived their usefulness should be disposed of."

The Baksh home was bought with a massive mortgage. Despite a joint income of nearly £90,000, Dr Baksh was in debt by 1983.

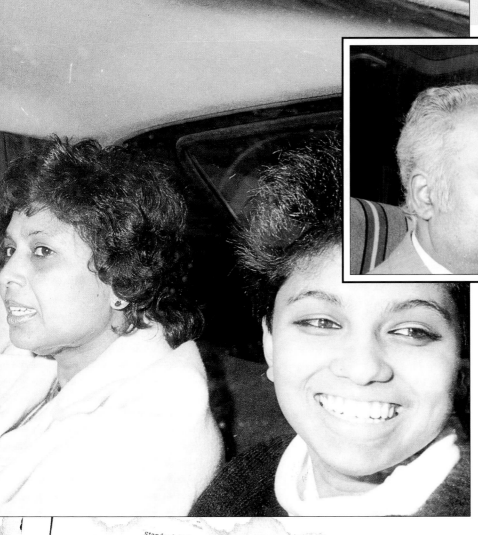

Above: Dr Baksh is driven away from the Old Bailey to start his life sentence. Mounting debts prompted him to buy a massive life insurance policy on his wife, and to plan a ruthless murder.

Left: Dr Madhu Baksh leaves court with her children. In addition to murdering his first wife, police had grave suspicions about the premature deaths of two of his fellow colleagues, Dr David Jones and Dr John Groome. Both had been fit men who suddenly collapsed and died. But their bodies had been cremated, making forensic tests impossible.

**The London Evening Standard
18 December 1986**

Standard Picture: A ... ART

MURDER GP GETS LIFE

'You killed to gratify your lust'

by Shekhar Bhatia
and Patrick McGowan

EVIL Dr John Baksh was found guilty this afternoon of murdering his first wife and attempting to kill the second.

Baksh was sentenced to life imprisonment on the first charge, with a recommendation that he serve a minimum of 20 years because of the danger he posed to his close family.

For the attempted murder of Dr Madhu

Baksh, his second wife, he was sentenced to 14 years.

The grey-haired Kent GP folded h's hands as if to pray and stumbled slightly as the jury returned its double verdict after two hours and five minutes.

Baksh, 53, was flanked by two prison officers in the dock for the verdict.

Sentencing him, the City of London Recorder, Sir James Miskin, said: "You intentionally killed your first wife when you knew she was both unwell and utterly miserable because she suspected you were carrying on with Madhu

"You killed her skilfully to gratify your lust for Madhu, and deprived your two young children of their mother.

"Nearl y three years later you injected Madhu as you had Ruby with morphine. You took her to Keston Ponds intending to kill her. You slit her throat and made it look as if some third party had done it."

He said it was only through sheer good luck and the skill of surgeons that she survived, but with her nec kterribly scarred in two places.

"I am satisfied that there was nothing which could possibly be described as provocative behaviour on the part of Madhu which could begin to justify the extent of your behaviour," said Sir James.

"It may well be that you long resented her disciplinary attitude towards your son, and stored up a powerful feeling of rese

He killed his first wife Ruby on a holiday in Spain. Ruby, who was also a doctor in their two Kent practices, at Nottingham and Bickley, was buried the day after her murder. Baksh flew back to Britain and into the arms of the woman he intended to morry, Dr Madhu Kumar.

The eight-day Old B

January this year he attempted to murder her by slitting her throat and injecting her with morphine.

She was discovered, barely alive, at Keston Ponds, Kent, later that night.

This afternoon she described her surviv!

a team at Bromley Hospital saved her life.

The Crown told the Old Bailey of a dramatic confession by the killer in August, 1983, in Paris when he broke down in tea

THE DOCTOR AND THE WIFE . . . John Baksh and Madhu who was lucky to survive h is attack.

The ruthless cruelty of Dr John Baksh stunned the Old Bailey court. His flimsy explanations could not withstand close scrutiny, and he was found guilty by a unanimous decision.

WEDGWOOD SALE
TWO TABLEWARE
rmal prices

THOMPSON AND BYWATERS

CRIME OF PASSION

The affair between Edith Thompson and Frederick Bywaters could only continue with the death of her husband.

At around midnight on 3 October 1922, Edith Jessie Thompson and her husband Percy were walking from Ilford station to their home in Kensington Gardens. They had been to London's Criterion Theatre to see the comedy *A Little Bit of Fluff*. Outwardly all seemed well; but under the surface deep resentments were seething. Percy Thompson didn't like his wife going out to work. He believed a wife's place was in the home, cooking, ironing and raising children. And that was another resentment: Percy wanted children, Edith did not.

Earlier that day Mrs Thompson had met her lover, Frederick Bywaters, eight years her junior, in the teashop opposite Carlton & White, a wholesale milliners where she was manageress. She used her maiden name, Graydon, in business and earned £6 a week (which was more than her husband earned as a clerk).

Husband stabbed

As Edith and Percy reached De Vere Gardens and Endsleigh Gardens, along Belgrave Road, Bywaters sprang out of the shadows, stabbed Thompson in the neck several times, and then ran off.

A short time later Dora Pittard and Percy Clevely, who were with a group of friends, saw a near-hysterical Mrs Thompson calling to them: "Oh, my God! Will you help me? My husband is ill, he is bleeding."

Pittard and Clevely summoned Dr Maudsley, who lived nearby. He examined Thompson and found he had been dead for about 10 minutes. Mrs Thompson, in an agitated, confused state, said "Why did you not come sooner and save him?"

An examination by the police surgeon at

Lovers Edith Thompson and Frederick Bywaters were two parts of a tragic marital triangle.

The Crime

Murder in the street

As Percy and Edith Thompson walked along Ilford's solidly middle-class Belgrave Road after a night at a West End theatre, violence seemed far from their minds. Suddenly, a man leaped from the shadows, brandishing a knife. Edith was pushed aside and was stunned as her head hit a wall. When she came to, her husband Percy lay dying in the street.

Percy Thompson died within minutes of being stabbed at this spot on Belgrave Road, Ilford.

Frederick Bywaters disposed of the cheap knife he had used down a drain, from where it was later recovered.

the local mortuary the next morning revealed that Thompson had several stab wounds to the face and neck, one of which had resulted in the severing of the carotid artery.

At first Mrs Thompson denied knowing who her husband's killer was; but under keen questioning by Scotland Yard's Chief Superintendent Frederick Wensley and Detective Inspector Sellars she began to talk of Frederick Bywaters, her lover of 18 months. "Oh God! Oh God! What can I do?" she said. "Why did he do it? I did not want him to do it. I must tell the truth."

When arrested, Bywaters coolly told Wensley and Sellars that he knew nothing about any murder and that he had learned of Thompson's death from the evening paper. But once he was told that Mrs Thompson had made a confession naming him as her husband's murderer, Bywaters admitted stabbing Percy Thompson with a sheath knife.

'Eternal triangle'

On the face of it, it was an 'eternal triangle' and as old as the hills – an ordinary case of a jealous man killing the husband of a woman with whom he was having an affair. Except that the protagonist of this deadly drama – Edith Thompson – was far from ordinary. In the words of her defence counsel, Sir Henry Curtis-Bennett, she was "one of the most extraordinary personalities" he had ever met.

The seeds of the affair were sown in early summer, 1921. The Thompsons went on holiday to Shanklin on the Isle of Wight with Edith's sister, Avis, and 19-year-old Bywaters, a family friend. Bywaters had known Edith's family, the Graydons, since

his schooldays. He had lived with the family in Manor Park for a time after his father was killed in World War I.

On leaving school, Bywaters got a job with a firm of shipping agents, and by 1918 he had become a ship's clerk on the P & O Line's steamer *Morea*.

But what had once been an innocent friendship now, during that Isle of Wight holiday, became a blind passion. Lying on the beach Bywaters – 12 years younger than Edith's dull, pernickerty husband – regaled her with stories of his travels to exotic ports around the world. The attraction between the young, robust traveller and the wife bored by her unimaginative husband quickly grew.

The unsuspecting Thompson readily agreed to Edith's suggestion that Bywaters should rent their spare room at 41 Kensington Gardens. The cosy arrange-

ment did not last long, however. Within weeks Thompson quarrelled with Edith over her liking for Bywaters "to run all your errands and obey all your requests". The row turned violent. And when Bywaters intervened, Thompson gave him his marching orders.

Love letters

Bywaters returned to his mother's house in Westow Street, Upper Norwood, until September, when his ship sailed for Australia. It was then that Mrs Thompson wrote the first of 65 letters to Bywaters, all of which he kept.

Right: Detectives asked Frederick Bywaters, a close friend of the Thompsons, to come down to Ilford police station to see if he could shed any light on the murder. Edith was being questioned at the time, denying all knowledge of the killer. But when she saw her lover, she broke down and accused him of the murder. As a result, Bywaters was charged.

The eternal triangle

"**D**arlingest lover of mine, thank you, thank you, oh thank you a thousand times for Friday – it was lovely – it's always lovely to go out with you.

"And then Saturday – yes I did feel happy – I didn't think a teeny bit about anything in this world, except being with you – and all Saturday evening I was thinking about you . . . feeling all the time how much I had won – cos I have darlint, won such a lot – it feels such a great big thing to me sometimes – that I can't breathe
. . .

"Darlingest lover, what happened last night? I don't know myself I only know how I felt – no not really how I felt but how I could feel – if time and circumstances were different."

Edith Thompson to Frederick Bywaters, September 1922

Frederick, Edith and Percy relax in the garden. Handsome and well travelled, Bywaters was a total contrast to Edith's dull husband.

Thirty of those letters – the ones selected by the prosecution as helpful to their case – were to be the pivot of the Crown's evidence against Mrs Thompson. The prosecution produced not a shred of proof that she knew in advance that Bywaters was going to kill her husband, nor that she knew that Bywaters was lying in wait for them on the fateful night.

Leading for the prosecution the Solicitor-General, Sir Thomas Inskip's aim was to show, from Mrs Thompson's own words, that the lovers' intention was to end Percy Thompson's "rights" by conspiring together to bring about his death. And the cumulative effect of her letters to Bywaters became more and more damaging as the trial progressed.

In some letters Mrs Thompson enclosed newspaper cuttings she thought "might prove interesting" – a curate who, mysteriously, had been poisoned to death by hyoscine; a case of 'Ground Glass In Box', and 'Deadly Powder Posted to Oxford Chancellor', and 'Girl's Death Riddle'.

Pretty but extremely vain, Edith Thompson saw herself as a woman of destiny. Unusually for the time, she had a responsible job managing a millinery firm. This was a bone of contention with her husband, who felt that a woman's place was in the home.

Handsome Frederick Bywaters called himself a seaman, although he was actually a sea-going clerk. His tales of travel to exotic places enthralled Edith. She thought that he was the knight in shining armour who would rescue her from her humdrum existence.

Bitter-tasting tea

But most damaging of all was a reference to Percy Thompson complaining of his Sunday morning tea tasting bitter "as if something had been put in it".

Mrs Thompson adds: "Now I think whatever else I try it in again will still taste bitter – he will recognise it and be more suspicious, and if the quantity is still not successful it will injure any chance I may have of trying when you come home."

She also appears to suggest she had been feeding her husband broken glass: "I'm going to try the glass again – when it is safe. I used the 'light bulb' three times, but the third time – he found a piece."

Though the letters were damning by implication, they were not proof that Mrs Thompson had actually given her husband poison or any harmful substance. In the hope of getting that proof the prosecution had ordered the exhumation of Percy Thompson's body, and assigned the postmortem to Sir Bernard Spilsbury, the Home Office pathologist.

But Spilsbury found no trace of any poison, and no traces of the passage through the body of pieces of glass or powdered electric light bulbs. Spilsbury's analyst, Dr John Webster, confirmed his findings.

Unlike Mrs Thompson, Bywaters had no arguable defence. Giving evidence, he said he had stabbed Thompson because he thought the man had a gun and was going to shoot him. Thompson had said: "I've got her. I'll keep her and I'll shoot you."

Bywaters added that Thompson had struck him in the chest, then reached towards his pocket. He, Bywaters, had then stabbed Thompson "in self-defence".

"Any right-minded person will be filled with disgust"

Mr Justice Shearman's moralistic summing up at the end of the trial left no-one in any doubt about his feelings.

"We are told", he said, "that this is a case of great love. Gentlemen, if this nonsense means anything, it is that the love of a husband for his wife is something improper, and that the love of a woman for her lover, illicit and clandestine, is something great and noble. I am certain that you, like any other right-minded persons, will be filled with disgust at such a notion."

Shearman went on to imply – in fact, he all but directed the jury to believe – that because of her loose morals, Edith was just the sort of evil woman who would arrange the murder of her husband.

To his credit, Bywaters did his best to avoid incriminating Edith Thompson.

Then Mrs Thompson went into the witness box. Her counsel had strongly advised her against doing so, but she stubbornly insisted. It was a fatal mistake; what sympathy she might have had, what doubts the jury might have harboured about her complicity in the murder, were quickly dispelled by her own words. For however much she might have felt for the besotted Bywaters, it didn't stop her from trying to save her own skin by putting the full blame on him. That, too, was to go against her.

Though she had been her own worst enemy in the witness box, Curtis-Bennett's address to the jury did much to redress the balance. "This is not an ordinary charge of murder," he told them. "These are not ordinary people you are trying. Am I right or wrong in saying that this woman is one of the most extraordinary personalities that you or I have ever met?"

If her letters showed anything, he said, it was that she was telling Bywaters that she would go to any lengths to hold his affection – "They certainly do not make her a principal to the killing of Thompson."

Guilty of murder

But Mr Justice Shearman took the opposite view, describing Mrs Thompson's letters as being "full of the outpourings of a silly but, at the same time, wicked affection." His summing up, overlaid by his moralist views, left the jury in no doubt that he believed Mrs Thompson and Bywaters were guilty of murder.

But he did not mention the fact that no glass or poison had been found in Thompson's body. Nor did he remind the jury of

The Evening News
London's Predominant Evening Journal. Largest Evening Net Sale in the World

LONDON : FRIDAY, JANUARY 5, 1923.

FORTY-SECOND YEAR.

NO. 12,827.

ONE PENNY.

ILFORD MURDERERS : NO REPRIEVE—Official.

MRS. THOMPSON & BYWATERS TO BE HANGED ON TUESDAY.

AR LAW COMES HOME.

SMILES WITH

THE PRINCE OF WALES.

Official Denial of Any Engagement.

DOWN 75FT. CLIFF TO SAVE A DOG.

Fire Chief's Thrilling Rescue in the Darkness.

MRS. THOMPSON.   FREDERICK BYWATERS.

The following Official Announcement was issued by the Office this afternoon :—

WHITE STAR AND SOVIET.

"WHO SAID 'BURGLARS'!"

Over a million signed a petition for the reprieve of Edith Thompson, but they were ignored by the Home Secretary. He may have been influenced by an even stronger popular feeling, fanned up by the press, that the adulterous villainess was only getting what she deserved.

Below: The lovers were condemned to die. Bywaters accepted his guilt, but Edith's outburst showed that she had expected her lover to take all the blame.

Mrs Thompson's capacity for make-believe or the possibility that she invented many of things she said in her letters to Bywaters.

It took the jury two and a quarter hours to reach a guilty verdict on both.

When the death sentence was passed Mrs Thompson cried: "I am not guilty! Oh my God, I am not guilty!"

Bywaters and Mrs Thompson appealed against the verdict before the Court of Criminal Appeal, but the Lord Chief Justice decided the case had been clearly put before the jury. He described the case as "a squalid and indecent case of lust and adultery" and Mrs Thompson's letters as "remarkable and deplorable . . . full of the most mischievous and perilous stuff."

A national daily newspaper organised a petition on Mrs Thompson's behalf; though it was signed by more than a million readers, the Home Secretary did not grant a reprieve.

On the morning of 9 January 1923, Edith Thompson went to the scaffold at Holloway Prison and Bywaters was hanged at Pentonville Prison. As her counsel Curtis-Bennett said afterwards, "Mrs Thompson was hanged for immorality."

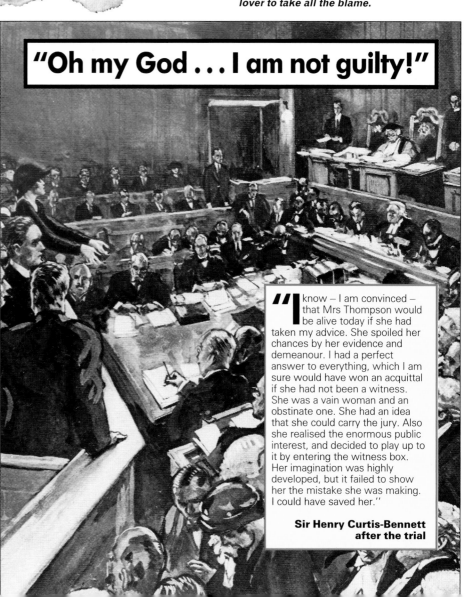

"Oh my God . . . I am not guilty!"

"I know – I am convinced – that Mrs Thompson would be alive today if she had taken my advice. She spoiled her chances by her evidence and demeanour. I had a perfect answer to everything, which I am sure would have won an acquittal if she had not been a witness. She was a vain woman and an obstinate one. She had an idea that she could carry the jury. Also she realised the enormous public interest, and decided to play up to it by entering the witness box. Her imagination was highly developed, but it failed to show her the mistake she was making. I could have saved her."

Sir Henry Curtis-Bennett after the trial